ESCAPIN

What to Expect When You Divorce a narc

David E. Clarke, Ph.D.

Copyright 2023 David Clarke

All rights reserved. The author guarantees all contents are original and do not infringe upon the legal rights of any other person or work. No part of this book may be used or reproduced, stored in a retrieval system or transmitted in any form or by any means without prior permission of the author, except in the case of brief quotations embodied in critical articles and reviews.

ISBN 978-0-578-27940-4

Printed in the United States of America

INTRODUCTION

You Have Had Enough

You have officially had enough of the narcissist you married. Enough of all the pain and misery and destruction the narc has unleashed on you and your children.

You Have Had More Than Enough

You have had more than enough of your spouse's:

Refusing to meet your needs

Extreme selfishness

Refusing to create intimacy

Refusing to talk about difficult topics

Refusing to talk about anything he doesn't want to talk about

Silent treatment for days and weeks, even months

Gaslighting

Manipulating

Extreme mood shifts

Stonewalling

Guilting

Blaming you for everything

Isolating you from family and friends

Projecting

Verbal abuse

Constant criticism

Mocking

Degrading

Superior attitude

Need to control

Lies that never end

Character assassinating you behind your back

Inability to ever be wrong about anything

Indifference

Zero empathy

Zero conscience

Passive-aggressiveness

Playing the victim

Unpredictable rages (and maybe physical violence)

Lecturing

Ranting

Demanding sex

Denying you sex

Unreasonable, irrational jealousy

Spotlight seeking

Addictions

False promises

Fake apologies

Hypocrisy

Fake spirituality

Alienating your children

(and this isn't a complete list)

Your Spouse is a Monster

    This isn't just a lousy husband, even though he is a lousy husband. This isn't just a husband with whom you can't create intimacy, even though you can't create intimacy with him. This isn't just a husband you are very unhappy with, even though you are very unhappy with him.

This is a full blown narcissist. An abusive monster who is destroying you and your children.

If you still wonder if your spouse is a narcissist (and my above list of 41 traits of a narc isn't enough to convince you), read the first 6 chapters of my book, *Enough is Enough: A Step-by-Step Plan to Leave an Abusive Relationship with God's Help.*

You Have Tried and Tried and Tried . . .

Over the years, you have done what all good Christian spouses have done: you have tried everything-and I mean everything-to help the narc change.

Prayer. Talking to your pastor. Counseling. Marriage seminars. Marriage intensives. Books. Continuing to love him and meet his needs while he was emotionally beating you to death. Twisting yourself into someone you don't even recognize in a desperate attempt to tolerate his never-ending abuse. Crying. Begging. Pleading.

Nothing has worked. There has been no change in the narc. Or, he's worse.

You Get It Now

It took years, but you get it now. You understand narcissism and the awful damage the narc has done to you and your precious kids.

One of my phone advice clients told me, "I have a Ph.D. in narcissism." I replied, "Yes, you do, and you've earned it the hard way."

You realize what most in the Christian community will never realize: the narc won't change. He'll keep abusing you until there's nothing left of you. And nothing left of your children.

99.9 % of narcs won't change. Yes, you read that correctly. In his crazy head, the narc has done absolutely nothing wrong. It's all your fault.

His core of sinful pride prevents any admission of fault, any humility, any vulnerability, so change isn't an option.

Divorce is Not What You Wanted

You wanted a happy marriage and family. You wanted the narc to change. You wanted healing and restoration.

You spent years fighting to improve your marriage. Fighting to stay married.

That fight is over. There will be no restoration of the marriage. But there will be restoration of you and your children and your children's children. In fact, the only way restoration can happen is by divorcing the narc.

No one else but you and God and a few diehard supporters (and maybe your older children) realize what you have suffered. But that's enough.

You are not taking a vote on whether or not to file divorce. In the Christian community, the vote would be: don't file.

The only vote that counts is God's vote. And God wants you out of this marriage and free.

You Have a Biblical Reason to Divorce

There are three biblical reasons to divorce:

1. Abandonment by a nonChristian spouse (1 Corinthians 7:15a).

2. Adultery (Matthew 19:7-9).

3. Chronic abuse-emotional and/or physical (1 Corinthians 7:15b).

Because your spouse is a narcissist, you have the third reason. No question. You may also have one of the other two reasons, but you certainly have the third reason: chronic abuse.

For my complete explanation of the three biblical reasons for divorce, read my book: *I Didn't Want a Divorce, Now What?*

God Has Released You From The Marriage

One of my YouTube subscribers put it this way: "God called me out of my marriage." After hearing her story of years of abuse by the narc, I agreed.

Just as God called the Israelites out of Egypt-out of captivity and abuse and misery-He has called you out of your abusive marriage.

God released the Israelites from their abusers and He has released you from your abuser.

It's Time to Save Yourself

You are saving yourself. You are saving your children. You have a biblical right to file.

The narc has destroyed the marriage. You are only formalizing what he has already done.

God loves you and your children and He wants the horror and the trauma to stop.

This is War

Being married to an abusive narc is a nightmare. Divorcing one is another nightmare.

The narc wants to win. He wants to maintain control. He wants to make you suffer. He wants to turn your children against you. He wants everyone to think you're a bad person. He wants to leave you with no money and no assets.

THE NARC WANTS TO DESTROY YOU.

This divorce process will be a war. It will go on longer than you want. It will be more painful than you can imagine. It will cost much more-financially-than you expect.

It will be a vicious, nasty, emotionally and physically and spiritually draining, all out war.

My goal in this book is to get you ready for the war and guide you through it. To transform you into a warrior.

Knowledge is Power

This is your field manual for the divorce war. It is based on the experiences of abused spouses who have survived a divorce with a narc: my phone advice clients and subscribers to all my social media platforms. (YouTube, TikTok, Facebook, Instagram, and my podcast)

The more you know about what is coming, the better prepared you'll be. I'll tell you what the narc will do. I'll tell you what many in the Christian community will do. I'll tell you what the legal system will do.

And I'll tell you what you can do to survive the war. No one wins in a divorce. But you and your children need to survive it.

My Credentials

I've been a practicing Christian psychologist for over 35 years. I have a Ph.D. in clinical psychology and a master's degree in biblical studies. I use God's truth in the Bible and God's truth in psychology in my work.

Target Audience

If you're going through a divorce with an abusive narc-no matter who filed-this book is for you.

The narc can be a husband or a wife. For ease of communication and to avoid the awkward he/she routine, I'll refer to the husband as the narc. But, all these principles apply to a female narc as well.

As you have noticed, I will use the word narc for narcissist throughout this book. Small n, because the narc doesn't deserve a capital n. He is a small, pathetic person and so deserves a small n.

And it will be *the* narc, not *your* narc, because he's no longer your narc.

My Divorce War Plan

My plan has five parts.

Part One: The Decision That Starts the War

You don't have to stay married and you need to not waver from your decision to divorce.

Part Two: The Declaration of War

Your team of warriors, what to do before you file, and how to communicate with the narc after you file.

Part Three: The Personal War

The many ways the narc will attack you and what you can do about it.

Part Four: The Parental War

The many ways the narc will try to alienate your children and what you can do about it.

Part Five: The Legal War

The many ways the narc will attack you legally and what you can do about it.

God is With You

He lifted me out of the slimy pit, out of the mud and mire; he set my feet on a rock and gave me a firm place to stand. He put a new song in my mouth . . . (Psalm 40:2-3)

You have to spend time in the slimy pit, in the mud and mire. But God will set your feet on a rock and put a new song in your mouth.

God sees you. God hears you. God knows the pain and trauma you have suffered from the narc. God knows how hard you tried in your marriage.

God loves you and wants you to be free. God is with you and will remain with you as you go through the divorce.

Now, let me show you how to survive this divorce.

CHAPTER ONE

You Don't Have to Stay Married to a Monster

But mark this: There will be terrible times in the last days. People will be lovers of themselves, lovers of money, boastful, proud, abusive, disobedient to their parents, ungrateful, unholy, without love, unforgiving, slanderous, without self-control, brutal, not lovers of the good, treacherous, rash, conceited, lovers of pleasure rather than lovers of God-having a form of godliness but denying its power. Have nothing to do with them. (2 Timothy 3:1-5)

Have you ever read a better description of an abusive narc? I haven't. These are the apostle Paul's words, written with the power and guidance of God.

You Are Married to a 2 Timothy 3:1-5 narc

These verses describe who you are married to. You have decided-finally-to follow the clear instructions at the end of this description of a narc: "Have nothing to do with them."

Paul does not advise you to give narcs like these another chance. He gives no indication that these types of narcs will ever change. They are evil and dangerous and you need to get away from them.

Living in the narc's Reality

The narc has his own reality. He lives in his own world. It's Bob's world. Or, Susie's world.

He makes all the rules. He is the King. For all intents and purposes, he is his own god.

What you think, what you feel, and what you need makes no difference. It is meaningless to him. All that counts is what *he* thinks, what *he* feels, and what *he* needs.

Living in his reality, making constant adjustments to survive in his reality, has cost you dearly. It has been a horrific mix of rejection and never-ending emotional torture.

You are wounded. You are traumatized. You have PTSD (Post Traumatic Stress Disorder). Your immune system is trashed because of the unrelenting stress. You have depression and anxiety. You have experienced humiliation, helplessness, and hopelessness for years.

You have lost yourself. You can't remember who you used to be.

Your body, mind, and soul are dying.

One of my TikTok subscribers told me: "Slowly dying is worse than starting over."

The Marriage is Over

Why does the Bible give the three reasons for divorce? Because any of these behaviors- abandonment by a nonChristian spouse, adultery, and chronic abuse-inflicts a catastrophic, fatal wound to a marriage.

Any one of these sinful behaviors ends a marriage. It's over. It is completely destroyed.

The narc and other clueless persons will urge you to not end the marriage. They are mistaken. The narc has already ended the marriage with his outrageous, damaging behavior. You had nothing to do with it.

As much as God values marriage, He despises these three sinful actions and makes it clear they are reasons to divorce.

It is possible to fully heal and recover from these awful wounds. And, build a brand new, healthy, intimate marriage.

Over the years, I have helped many married couples-hundreds and hundreds-do just that. *But not when one of the spouses is an abusive narc who has been given a million chances to repent and has chosen not to every time.* Marriage counseling with an abusive narc in the room is a waste of time.

The point is, you don't have to work on the marriage. God does not say you have to. God says if you have one or more of these reasons, you can formally end a marriage that your spouse has already killed.

Do You Want to Please Others or God?

You can stay married to the narc. That's your choice. I've had many abused clients choose to stay.

Just about every single one has regretted it.

Why? Because most narcs don't change and the destruction continues. Oh, the narc may "change" for a few weeks. Maybe a few months. But he'll go back to his abusive ways. How many times has he done this to you?

So, you can stay married and please the Peanut Gallery of pastors, friends, and family who want you to stay. (more on these types in a later chapter)

But who cares what these misguided fools think? They don't live with the narc. They have no idea the suffering you and your children have experienced. It is worth your life to please them?

The one person you want to please is God. And God is not pleased when you stay with the narc. How could He be pleased when you and your kids continue to be broken, piece by piece?

What if the narc Actually Changes?

Even if the narc truly repents and changes (and frankly, that is highly unlikely), you can decide-biblically-you don't want to stay married to him.

Your heart, mind, body, and soul have taken enough of a beating.

Your decision to divorce is okay. It's okay with God. He knows the nightmare of abuse you have suffered.

Nothing in Scripture tells you that you have to stay married to a person when you have a biblical reason to divorce him.

You don't have to endure the incredible stress and pressure of living with the narc and waiting, every day for the rest of your life, for him to go back to his abusive behavior.

You will heal from the wounds the narc inflicted on you. You will forgive him. But you don't have to trust him for one more second. You don't!

You don't have to be open and vulnerable to him ever again.

Finally, It's Not About the narc

It's always been about the narc. Your whole relationship has been about the narc. You haven't mattered to him-not even a little bit.

It's no longer about him. Now, it's about you. Your healing, your peace, your happiness, your freedom. Your new life.

And it's about your children. Their healing, their peace, their happiness, their freedom, and their new lives.

One of my phone advice clients wrote me these words: "I embraced the feeling of being free. Everything looked so much brighter. I could enjoy the sky, trees, flowers, birds . . . the simple things. Everything came alive again, including me."

The freedom she's talking about is worth the war you have to go through to achieve it.

CHAPTER TWO

Do Not Waver

By filing, you are making a frontal assault on the narc's view of himself. Nothing is more precious to him than his view of himself.

"I am Perfect"

The narc sees himself as perfect. He's not just smarter than you-he's smarter than everyone. He is simply incapable of mistakes. He is a wonderful, special person.

"No, You're Not Perfect"

With the filing, you are telling him and the entire world he is not perfect. You are rejecting him because he has wounded you deeply with his abusive behavior.

The narc will do all he can to maintain his image-to himself, your children, family members, church leaders, friends, and everyone he knows.

Why the narc Wants to Stop the Divorce

The narc wants you to stop the divorce. Not because he loves you. He loves only himself.

Not because he realizes how he has damaged you. He couldn't care less. If you are damaged, it's your fault.

Not because he intends to spend eight months to a year working to change. Are you kidding? You don't change when you're perfect.

He wants you to stop the divorce because he wants to:

- Take control back from you
- Buy time so he can figure out how to keep more of his money
- Work on the kids so they'll turn on you
- Look good to the kids, family, friends, your pastor, the community
- Discredit all you are saying about him

If You Change Your Mind

If you pause the divorce or cancel it, you will pay a horrendous price. Your position that he is an abusive narc who has wounded you deeply for years is wiped out. Gone.

Your credibility is shattered. No one will believe what you say about him from now on.

The narc will gleefully say to others, including your children: "If I'm so abusive and so bad, why did she pause the divorce? Why did she cancel it? Why is she going to marriage counseling with me?"

He will make you out to be a liar. And he'll be convincing. And it will be your own fault.

If You Waver, The Abuse Gets Worse

If you are foolish enough to waver, even if you don't take him back, he'll "try" for a few weeks, maybe a few months, and then go back to his true self. His abusive self.

(As you read these words, if you still have doubts about the divorce decision and feel guilty, get my book: *20 Lies That Keep You With Your Abuser.* This book will empower you and enable you to shred your codependency.)

The narc will become even more abusive to you because you had the nerve to file. Far from being happy you gave him yet another chance, he will never forgive you for filing. Never.

He will never stop making you suffer for filing.

Don't despair if you have made the mistake of wavering in your decision to divorce. Get back on track legally. Move forward with the divorce.

Do what you can to repair the damage to your credibility, especially with your kids. Explain why you wavered, apologize for doing so, and encourage the kids to talk through their feelings about it.

Assure your children and support team that you will not change your mind again.

You might lose some support team members because you disappointed them and lost their trust. So be it. Get new support team members.

CHAPTER THREE

Get Ready for the Lovebomber

There are plenty of narcs(the obvious, overt types)who will go into vicious attack mode the moment you file.

But most narcs-overt and covert-will immediately launch into a two stage offensive after the filing: lovebombing followed by fake repentance.

Let's look at lovebombing first.

Beware a Liar and a Flatterer

A lying tongue hates those it hurts, and a flattering mouth works ruin. (Proverbs 26:28)

The narc has always been a liar. He's lied about everything, even the most trivial of matters. Now, he'll take his lying to a new level. His entire lovebombing campaign is nothing but a pack of lies. Pretty lies. Lovely lies. But lies nonetheless.

The narc has always flattered you. To make up for sinful behavior. To distract you from his abuse. To get what he wants. To get sex.

Now, he'll take his flattery to a masterful level of performance art. No one who ever lived will flatter like he's going to flatter you.

Same Old, Same Old

You've been here before with the narc. He has deja vued you over and over again with his lovebombing.

He has used this narc technique to move quickly past conflicts (that he created), make sure there is no discussion of the problems, and get you to forgive him and move on.

Which is what you have always done. But, the pouring out of his "love" never lasts, does it? Once he gets what he wants, the love stops and the abuse resumes.

It won't last this time, either.

Love, Niagara Falls Style

After you file, the narc will initiate a massive amount of lovebombing. Industrial strength lovebombing. World-class lovebombing. It will be as if you are standing under Niagara Falls, drowning in an intensely powerful torrent of love.

To anyone who doesn't know the real narc (which is everyone but you), it will be undeniable that this man truly loves you.

How could you miss it? What's the matter with you? Why won't you give this amazing lover another chance?

The Desires of Your Heart

The narc actually knows your deepest desires and needs in the marriage. Up to now, he hasn't cared. The truth is, he still doesn't care, but he's smart enough to make promises to stop you from divorcing him.

Spiritual

"I'll become a Christian. I'll grow in my faith. I'll go to church with you. I'll pray with you. I'll do devotions with you."

Romantic

"I'll date you on a regular basis. I'll spend time with you. We'll take trips together."

Communication

"I'll open up and talk. I'll share my personal thoughts and feelings. I'll listen to you."

Financial

"We'll make money decisions together. You'll have full access to all the money. We'll fix the home. We'll remodel the home. We'll buy a new home. We'll buy you a new car. We'll pay for the education and training you've been asking for."

Parenting

"I'll support you as a parent. We'll be a team in raising the kids. I'll spend time with the kids. We'll have regular family time. I'll pay for private Christian school. I'll pay for their sports and activities."

Everything you've always dreamed of for your marriage. Offered to you with absolute and convincing sincerity, since he is a wonderful liar who believes his own lies.

Don't fall for it.

A Second Courtship

Remember how he wooed you to get you to marry him? Remember how all that wooing stopped soon after the wedding?

The narc will woo you all over again in this lovebombing phase of his please stop the divorce strategy.

He'll communicate beautiful, romantic, sweet, and-apparently-heartfelt words to you. Words you've wanted to hear for years.

He'll say these loving things in person, over the phone, in voicemail messages, in love letters, in cards, in texts, and in emails.

He'll beg and plead and promise to change. For Heaven's sake, he's already changed! Can't you see that? He will spend the rest of his life (or, until you drop the divorce, whichever comes first), loving you and treating you like a queen.

Don't fall for it.

"Where was This Guy During Our Marriage?"

Interesting, isn't it? During the marriage, he gave you none of what you needed. Or, for only very brief periods of time.

The narc spent years spitting on your marriage. Rejecting you. Tearing you to pieces.

Now, he says he loves you. He loves your marriage. He loves his children. He can't go on without you. (You're tempted to say to this last statement: "Promise?")

You'd like to ask the narc (but don't bother): "If you knew what I needed all along, why didn't you act this way during the marriage?"

If you did ask this question (which I don't want you to), the narc would immediately reply, "Because I have finally seen the light."

All he's seen is how much the divorce will cost him-in money mostly, but also in reputation and loss of control.

Don't fall for it.

It's a Con

This avalanche of "love" means nothing. He hasn't changed, not even a little bit. He has no intention of changing. His only goal is to stop the divorce and wound you as you have never been wounded before.

He wants you to believe that all these promises, all this love, means he has changed. All it means is that he's trying to convince you-and others important to him-that he has changed.

Most narcs, post filing, will lovebomb for one or two months. Then they'll drop it. But I have seen narcs lovebomb for eight, nine, even ten months.

Whatever. Don't fall for it.

It's an act. It's all fake. It's a con.

If you fall for it and give him another chance, he'll make your life a living Hell just a few months down the road.

His abuse will be worse than ever.

CHAPTER FOUR

Get Ready for Mr. Repentance

If the narc's lovebombing doesn't work, he will shift into the next phase of his please don't divorce me plan: Mr. Repentance.

Often, the lovebombing and repentance overlap and occur at the same time.

Beware a Hypocrite

"Woe to you, teachers of the law and Pharisees, you hypocrites! You are like whitewashed tombs, which look beautiful on the outside but on the inside are full of dead men's bones and everything unclean. In the same way, on the outside you appear to people as righteous but on the inside you are full of hypocrisy and wickedness." (Matthew 23:27-28)

The narc has always been a hypocrite. He's presented a wonderful picture to the outside world, while he's been an abuser in the home.

Now, he'll take his hypocrisy to a new level. He'll project humility, brokenness, and super spirituality to you and everyone you know. He (or she) will look like the next Mother Teresa.

Many persons will nominate him for sainthood. And they won't be kidding.

Here's the thing. None of it is true. None of it.

The Apology Tour

The moment he realizes you have filed, the narc undergoes an incredible transformation. He morphs into the most pain-wracked, grief-stricken, heartbroken, contrite, pathetic, repentant creature (and I do mean creature) in the history of planet Earth. Probably the Universe.

The narc will admit, through tears and anguish, all his mistakes. All his awful behavior. All his abuse of you. Many narcs will even go into detail about their abusive behavior.

He'll tell you he gets it now. Everything has suddenly become crystal clear to him. He will apologize over and over to you for how he has harmed you over the years.

It's amazing. He knows what he's done wrong. He knows exactly how he has hurt you. It hasn't mattered to him up to now, has it?

Acting Repentant Isn't Being Repentant

The truth is, it still doesn't matter to him. What matters to him is losing control, losing face, and losing money.

One phone advice client said to me, "I'm caught up in a twenty year Jedi mind game." I told her, "Get prepared for a super-charged Jedi mind game when you file."

Don't believe a word the narc says. Don't believe any of his actions, either. He knows how to act repentant, you have to give him that. He has no idea how to actually *be* repentant.

Most narcs won't last more than two months (and it will probably be closer to two weeks) as Mr. Repentance. Especially if you ignore his apology tour and stay on the divorce track. Which is what I want you to do.

What Mr. Repentance Will Do

You will be hit with a tsunami of apparently repentant actions. The narc will:

- Promise to do anything to keep you two together

- Promise to love you until the end of time
- Promise to fully support you financially
- Promise to let you have the kids as much as you want
- Often cry like a baby
- Have a super sad look on his face whenever you see him
- Spend more time with the kids than he ever has
- Say he is 100% responsible for the marriage problems
- Apologize to your kids, your family, and your friends
- Call himself a narcissist
- Read a ton of marriage books, maybe even mine
- Read the Bible every day
- Have devotions every day
- Attend church every week
- Meet with the pastor regularly
- Attend a men's group
- Attend Celebrate Recovery
- Leave your church so it's not awkward for you
- Start individual counseling
- Ask you to go to marriage counseling

Not Sorry

The list you just read is a bunch of boxes the narc will check. It is his attempt-and it's pretty impressive, especially to those who don't know the real him-to prove his repentance.

All these words, promises, and actions must mean he's repentant, right? Wrong. The narc is a great actor and a great box checker. What he isn't is repentant.

The narc isn't sorry. Not even a tiny bit. He can *act* sorry-obviously-but he can't actually *be* sorry. Sorry is not part of his nature. He has no conscience.

He's had so many opportunities for so many years to be sorry. Has he ever been truly sorry? No.

You have given him a million chances to be sorry and change. How many times has he said words, made promises, changed for a little while, and then gone back to his abusive ways? I thought so.

For the narc, saying he's sorry and checking these boxes means he's sorry. His sorry tour should be applauded by you and everyone. He should get a Sorry Parade right down Main Street.

Like the magician he is, he will cleverly put the focus on his extreme sorriness. This will distract everyone from his years of abusive behavior.

You'll be sorry if you buy his act of being sorry.

It's Still All About Him

It's always been all about him and it's still all about him. All his efforts to stop the divorce have nothing to do with anyone but him.

This is not the "godly sorrow" Paul describes in 2 Corinthians 7:10. Godly sorrow is permanent. It is the real thing. It leads to genuine change. It is all about God.

This is "worldly sorrow." Worldly sorrow is temporary. It is fake. It leads to no change. It is all about the narc.

He'll say his repentance is about God. It's not about God. It's about him looking good and not losing.

He'll say his repentance is about you. It's not about you. It's about stopping you from divorcing him.

"I am Suffering!"

The pain you have caused him by filing is far worse-in his mind-than any pain you have experienced living with him. He has no concept of the debilitating pain that led you to file.

In fact, the pain he is feeling is far worse than the pain anyone has ever suffered since the beginning of time. This man is in agony. Actually, he's not. He's acting like he is.

Most persons who see his pain will assume he is broken and repentant. They will not see his sinful, abusive behaviors. They will see only his pain.

Oh, he'll tell others about his abusive behaviors, but his pain will override his abuse in their minds. And that's exactly what he wants.

Don't Believe His Repentance Act

It's all an act. A con. A manipulation. A performance. It is masterfully done, but it is fake.

The narc's repentance act makes him look good. To himself, which is most important. To your children, whose hearts and minds he is trying to win over. To others he wants to impress, so they can put pressure on you. And to you.

He is playing on your emotions. On your empathy. On your compassion. On your dream of a happy marriage and family. On your desire to not be divorced. On your Christianity.

He pretends empathy, but has none. He promises you the world, but won't deliver. At least, not for long.

Stick to the divorce path. Give him no response to his Mr. Repentance performance. He is desperate for any response, even a negative one, because that will tell him he's having an impact on you.

Don't respond in any way. Not even: "No." Not even: "I'm not interested."

Ignore all his efforts to prove he's repentant.

He'll get his Sorry Parade, because he'll fool many persons. But you don't have to attend the parade.

CHAPTER FIVE

Get Ready for the Peanut Gallery of Fools

A particularly nasty part of the narc's Mr. Repentance act is rounding up others to put pressure on you.

He brainwashes these persons into believing he's truly repentant. Then he manipulates them to reach out to you to convince you to stop the divorce.

Well before you file, the covert narc already has just about everyone fooled into thinking he's a wonderful, caring, special person. So, they will easily buy his "repentance."

The overt, obvious narc will have to work a little harder to gain supporters, but he'll get it done. He'll turn on the charm, turn on the tears, and people will believe he's a changed man.

A PR Campaign for Fools

The narc will win over persons you value and trust and respect:

Your children

Your family

Your friends

Your pastor

Your coworkers

Your neighbors

Your counselor

    These fools, who become a key part of his narcissistic supply, will come after you one by one and try to persuade you to stop the divorce.

    He'll turn just about everyone in your community against you and your rash, sinful decision to divorce him. The snot-nosed kid down the street will say to you: "Why don't you give Mr. Bob a shot?"

    These clueless suckups will do his bidding and they won't even know they've been artfully manipulated. In fact, they'll feel righteous and morally superior as they confront you.

    He has created a world in which his destructive sins of abuse are no longer the issue. He's convinced everyone-just about everyone-that the only issue is your sinful decision to divorce him.

    Masterful. Diabolically clever. And selfish. And evil.

The Peanut Gallery of Fools

A fool finds no pleasure in understanding but delights in airing his own opinions. (Proverbs 18:2)

The narc is a consummate liar. A master manipulator. A world-class actor.

But, these persons he unleashes on you are still fools. They lack sense. They will not listen to you. They will not try to understand the pain and damage you have suffered.

The truth is right in front of them, in the form of an abused and betrayed person. But, they don't care. They side with the bad guy.

The Nuts in the Peanut Gallery

Here are the usual suspects in the please don't divorce him Peanut Gallery.

Those in NonAbusive Marriages

They have decent, loving spouses and have no concept of the abuse you have suffered.

Those Who Say "No Biblical Reason"

They are spiritual HOA members. Legalists who do not believe that chronic abuse is biblical grounds for divorce. They actually don't accept any reason for divorce.

Those Who Don't Believe in Narcissism

They believe this whole narcissism thing is way overblown. They believe there aren't that many narcissists. And, anyway, your repentant spouse certainly can't be a narcissist.

Those Married to narcs

They are being abused by their narcs and have decided to stay. So, you should stay too. The thought of you getting free threatens them and angers them.

Those Who are narcs Themselves

They can't see any problem with the narc. They side with one of their own.

Those Spiritual Leaders Who Blame You

Many pastors and church leaders find it easier to blame you than the narc. They're scared of the narc and prefer the safety of confronting you. They believe your act of filing is worse than anything your spouse has done. Don't be shocked when your church leaders do church discipline on you, not the narc. Leave this type of church immediately. Find a local pastor who understands narcissistic abuse and will support you in the divorce process.

All these fools don't care about you. Not in the least. They'll say they care. But they don't.

They care about:

- Their misguided opinions
- Pleasing the narc
- Agreeing with the rest of their buddies in the Peanut Gallery
- Avoiding the hard and messy job of supporting you through the divorce

The Peanuts the Gallery Will Throw at You

Here are the top ten stupid things the Peanut Gallery will tell you, along with my responses:

Stupid thing #1: The abuse wasn't that bad.

DC: It was that bad! That's why she's divorcing him.

Stupid thing #2: Even if the abuse was that bad, it's not a biblical reason for divorce.

DC: Yes, it is a biblical reason. Do your research.

Stupid thing #3: He said he was sorry.

DC: Who cares? Sorry won't heal her wounds. Sorry won't rebuild her trust and her broken heart. And he's not sorry, anyway.

Stupid thing #4: He is totally repentant.

DC: You are totally naïve. No, he's not. If he was, he wouldn't have sent you to tell her he's totally repentant. Even if he is, her biblical reason to divorce still applies.

Stupid thing #5: You need to forgive him and work on the marriage.

DC: Those are two completely separate operations. She will forgive him, but she won't work on the marriage. She doesn't have to. And, what marriage are you talking about? There is no marriage because he destroyed it.

Stupid thing #6: Give him another chance.

DC: She's given him countless chances. Just curious, how many more chances should she give him? Two? Five? Twenty?

Stupid thing #7: Stay for the children.

DC: One of the reasons she is divorcing him is for the children. She's saving them from the full impact of his abuse.

Stupid thing #8: He's admitted his mistakes.

DC: Those mistakes just about killed her. She's not going back for more.

Stupid thing #9: He's changed already.

DC: Seriously? Get an IQ test and a screen for dementia. Or, get a Ph.D. in clinical psychology like me so you know what you're talking about. Do you know how many times he's changed?

Stupid thing #10: God can change him.

DC: Of course God can. That's no longer her concern. God has changed her.

Your Response to the Peanut Gallery

I hope you enjoyed my above responses to the Peanut Gallery. They are meant to empower you and entertain you. But I don't want *you* to give any responses to these nitwits. Zero.

Ignore the Peanut Gallery. Make no attempt to convince them of the abuse. They don't care. They won't listen. They would send you back to your narc to be completely destroyed.

You don't have the time or the energy to dialogue with these ignorant fools. Take no phone calls. No in person meetings. Do not return texts or emails. If they knock on your door, don't open the door.

If a member of the Peanut Gallery accosts you in public, say nothing and walk away.

Follow what the Bible teaches:

Do not speak to a fool, for he will scorn the wisdom of your words. (Proverbs 23:9)

CHAPTER SIX

Your Human Warriors

In my book, *Enough is Enough,* I recommend building a support team to help you leave the narc. You need the same team to lean on as you go through the divorce war.

No Wimps, Pantywaists, or Fence Sitters

Every warrior in your army must be one hundred percent supportive of you and your decision to divorce. These warriors are on your side absolutely and completely. They are committed to fighting with you to the bitter end.

They will ignore the narc and his efforts to reach out to them. And he will try to get to them. They will have no contact with the narc-ever. They love you and they can't stand the creepy/loser/evil dirtball you are divorcing.

Your human warriors are described in this verse:

A friend loves at all times, and a brother is born for adversity. (Proverbs 17:17)

Your Attorney

In case you didn't know it, the legal system is a joke. There is no fairness, no logic, and no justice. Just about everyone in the system-judges, attorneys(including yours), social workers, Guardian Ad Litems, police-doesn't care about you.

All these persons care about is getting paid. It's your life. All it is to them is a job.

Because the legal system is a broken joke and you are up against a cruel and vindictive narc, you must choose the right family law attorney. (More on how to find the right attorney in The Legal War section)

Interview attorneys until you find one who is experienced, mean (that's right, mean), aggressive, and tough as nails. It can be a man or a woman. A get down in the gutter fighter. And one who understands how to do battle with a narc.

Don't worry about your attorney being a Christian. That's not important in the legal arena. In fact, it can be a liability. A nice, sweet, passive Christian attorney will lose every time.

If you have a passive, kind, wimpy attorney-Christian or not-fire him or her immediately and find a legal Attila the Hun.

The narc and his sleazeball attorney (and the narc always hires a sleazeball attorney) will throw every nasty trick in the book at you. The narc wants to win, to keep all his money, to make you suffer, and to ruin your life.

Your cold-hearted attorney will not hold your hand or care about your feelings. She isn't your Christian therapist or a friend. She will do her job, which is to get you through the legal system. Cut through all the red tape and manipulation tactics of the narc and his attorney. Get you a decent deal. Get you divorced.

Your ice in her veins attorney will cost a lot more than you want to spend. More than you can afford. Go into debt if you have to. She will also end up saving you more money-a lot more-than a mediocre, ineffective attorney.

Don't ever do a collaborative divorce with the narc. It's worse than a waste of time. It will cost you a fortune and you will lose.

Don't ever use the same attorney. The narc and your "mutual" attorney will shaft you.

Some of you have very little money and the narc may not have much money. You simply can't afford an expensive attorney. Contact County Services. Legal Aid. Your local Women's Center. Your local Domestic Violence Center. Ask the family law attorneys in your area (call every one if you have to) to take your case pro bono or for a greatly reduced price. It can't hurt to ask.

Find a local paralegal who will take your case. The paralegal can do a ton of legal work for you for far less than an attorney.

Your Family and Friends

Ask your family and friends for emotional support, money, help with your kids, food, transportation, job leads, and whatever else you need.

Do not ask the narc's family for anything. Blood goes with blood. Plus, they're probably as crazy and abusive as he is.

Your Pastor

Find a pastor-and it may not be the one you have now-who will provide spiritual support, financial support, and practical help for the needs of you and your kids.

Your Christian Therapist

If you can afford it, find a local Christian therapist who can help you and your kids get through the divorce. This isn't the time to do deeper work on the trauma of your abuse. That will come later, after the divorce is final.

During the divorce, use your therapist to eliminate any remaining codependent tendencies, stay righteously angry and strong, and manage the stress of divorcing a narc.

Your Small Group

Unlike your attorney and your Christian therapist, your small group is free. Most likely, your small group will be connected to a church. The love, feedback, camaraderie, prayer, emotional and spiritual support, accountability, and practical help will be invaluable.

It could be a home group, a Bible study group, a men's or women's group, or a twelve step group such as Celebrate Recovery or DivorceCare. Just make sure it's a Christ-centered small group, one that recognizes Jesus Christ as the "higher power."

CHAPTER SEVEN

Take Care of Yourself

In the divorce, you will have to do battle with many enemies:

- The narc, of course
- The narc's attorney
- The legal system
- The Peanut Gallery
- satan (small s)

You need to be as strong and healthy as possible to deal effectively with these enemies and get through the divorce.

Love Yourself

Jesus taught that part of the second greatest commandment is to love yourself:

"And the second is like it: 'Love your neighbor as yourself.'" (Matthew 22:39)

You love yourself when you take care of yourself. The truth is, no one else will do that. It's your job.

Physical Separation

If possible, physically separate from the narc. If you live with the narc during the divorce, he'll find ten thousand ways to torture you.

You'll have to be the one to leave. Most narcs won't leave the home. If the narc does leave, he won't be gone long. He'll "visit" whenever he wants and eventually move back in. Legally, he has the right to be in the home. Thanks, legal system.

Before you leave, use your attorney to work out the time schedule with the children and temporary financial support. Your attorney will protect your financial interest in the home.

If You Can't Leave the Home

If you can't leave, get out of the bedroom. Move into another bedroom or another room and put a lock on the door. If he breaks in, call the police.

In addition to physical detachment (out of the bedroom, no affection or sex), create emotional detachment from him. Do not communicate with him in person or on the phone. Ever. Use only text, email, or a special app your attorney recommends. And only communicate about necessary matters: the kids and their needs and schedules, bills, taxes, and emergencies.

Shun him, ignore him in every way you can. No personal time with him. Do not ride in a car with him. No family time with him present. Do not sit with him at any meeting or event: church, school, sports.

All birthdays and holidays are separate. You'll celebrate with your children without him present. He is free to celebrate these events with the kids on his own.

Do nothing for him. No touching or sex (have I mentioned that?). No laundry. No food prepared for him. If you make a meal, he can eat it but you won't talk to him at the table. No errands for him.

If the narc has a flat tire or a car accident and has the nerve to call you for help, ignore him. If he asks for any personal favor, ignore him. In the same way, you ask him for nothing. That's what your support team is for.

Your Body

Get a physical with your family doctor. Take the steps your doc recommends to stay healthy. Exercise regularly. Lose weight. Eat a decent diet.

Physical health will give you strength, stamina, energy, and confidence. You'll need these qualities in the divorce.

If you are really struggling with depression and anxiety and stress, join the club. It's perfectly normal in a divorce. If your family doc recommends medication for an emotional condition, do not hesitate to take it.

Say No a Lot

Say no to just about every form of service: church, charity, community, your kid's school . . . You need your energy and your time for yourself and your kids. This is only for this season of divorce.

Also, it's okay not to tithe during the divorce. God understands. You can get back to tithing after the divorce.

You may have to say no to homeschooling or private school for your kids. And, no to certain extra activities for your kids. This is survival time. The priority is taking care of yourself, taking care of your kids, saving money, and getting divorced.

Get Some Rest

Sunday needs to be a day off. At least, most of the day. Many people don't realize that keeping the Sabbath Day holy and resting on that seventh day of the week is one of the Ten Commandments. (Exodus 20:8-11)

So, on Sunday, go to church and worship. And, rest. Take this day off from the divorce war and all work-related activities.

Manage Your Fear

You will experience fear throughout the divorce. Everyone who divorces a narc will be fearful. Anxious. Panicked at times.

Here is Dr. Clarke's handy guide for fear:

Expect It

Do not be surprised by it. It's going to happen often.

Embrace It

Do not dread the fear. Let it come. Your attitude is: "bring it on."

Let It Wash Through You

Do not resist or fight the fear. That will make it worse. Let it come in and blow through you. You are a Palm tree in a hurricane. Because you don't have a big, intense reaction, your system will calm down more quickly.

Study It and Find the Lies

Observe the fear and identify the lies behind it. Fear is always fueled by lies: "I'm going to have a mental breakdown." "I can't think straight and will lose my job." "I'm losing my mind." "I won't survive this divorce." Calmly and firmly refute these lies.

Focus on the Bible

Read and meditate on some calming Bible passages: John 14:27, Philippians 4:7, Psalm 17:8-9.

CHAPTER EIGHT

Stay Close to God

You need the human warriors in your army. But your most important warrior is a supernatural one: God.

You won't survive this war without God. On your own, even with your human warriors, you will be crushed. Devastated. Broken.

You need God to sustain you through this brutal, all out war with the narc.

God's Promises to Those Who Love Him

"Because he loves me," says the Lord, "I will rescue him; I will protect him, for he acknowledges my name. He will call upon me, and I will answer him; I will be with him in trouble, I will deliver him and honor him." (Psalm 91:14-15)

If you love God and call upon Him during this war, He will:

- Rescue you
- Protect you
- Answer your prayers
- Be with you in the war

- Deliver you
- Honor you

You Must Know God

To get these six amazing benefits (and more!), you must have a personal relationship with God, through His son, Jesus Christ. This is what makes you a Christian.

There is one God, and that is the God of the Bible. There is one way to establish a relationship with God, and that is through His son, Jesus Christ.

Here is Jesus Christ, in His own words:

"I am the way, the truth, and the life. No one comes to the Father except through Me." (John 14:6)

A Christian is one who has recognized his need of a Savior and through trusting Christ has been forgiven. God sent Jesus to die for your sins-all the things you've done wrong-so that you can have a relationship with God.

This is what you must do to become a Christian:

For I delivered to you first of all that which I also received: how Christ died for our sins according to the Scriptures, was buried, rose again on the third day according to the Scriptures. (1 Corinthians 15:3-4)

When you believe these truths-Jesus died for your sins, He was buried, and He rose from the dead-you become a Christian. You have a personal relationship with God through His son.

Become a Christian Right Now

If you are not a Christian yet, I urge you to become one. You can begin your relationship with God through Jesus right now by saying the words of this brief prayer:

Dear God,

I know I am a sinner. I've made many mistakes and sinned in my life. I realize my sin separates me from You, a holy God.

I believe that Your son, Jesus Christ, died for my sins, was buried, and rose from the dead. I give my life to You now.

If you prayed this prayer-not just the words, but believed in your heart-you now know God as a Father, and He will be by your side, and carry you at all times as you fight this war.

If you're not ready to become a Christian, that's okay. Read the rest of this book and then circle back to this chapter. I think you'll realize your need for God.

Time with God Every Day

Have a daily personal quiet time with God. Read the Bible-just a few verses-and meditate on it. God's Word will empower you. Comfort you. Energize you. And give you hope.

In your personal quiet time, pray. Here's how I want you to pray.

Pray for These Things

Pray that God will:

- Give you righteous anger at the narc
- Give you emotional detachment from the narc
- Give you peace
- Protect you against the attacks of the devil (and his buddy, the narc)
- Give you healthy relationships with your children
- Give your children protection and strength
- Give you a job if you need one

- Give you the money you need
- Give your human warriors perseverance and commitment to you
- Give you legal success

Pray with honesty and directness to God. It's normal and healthy to wrestle with God and question Him during the divorce. Follow David's example in sharing your raw emotions with God. (Psalm 13 and 43)

Pray that God will deal harshly with the narc. David prayed for God to shame, confuse, and disgrace his enemies. (Psalm 40:14) David prayed that God would destroy his enemies. (Psalm 54:5)

Pray that God will thwart the narc's efforts to harm you and your children. Pray that God will make him pay dearly for his abuse.

There will be times when you won't know what to pray. That's normal, too. The Bible teaches us (Romans 8:26) that in extreme circumstances, the Holy Spirit will pray for us.

One of my YouTube subscribers-who was in the middle of a divorce with a narc- sent me this email message: "Dave, I poured my heart out in prayer, sometimes screaming, often crying, sometimes groaning because no words would come."

This is a Spiritual Battle

satan will attack you with everything he has in his arsenal. (Ephesians 6:12) Just like the narc, he wants to destroy you. satan will do all he can, through the narc and his own lies, to harm you.

satan is ". . . a liar and the father of lies." (John 8:44) He is a better liar than even the narc. Be prepared for his lies and respond-out loud- assertively. Here are some lies of satan and responses you can shove down his throat:

satan: You are sinning by divorcing your spouse.

You: No, I'm not. Read 1 Corinthians 7:15

satan: Your mistakes harmed the marriage.

You: Partly true. My first mistake was marrying the dirtball. I also tolerated his abuse far too long. But my mistakes didn't destroy the marriage. His mistakes, his abuse, did.

satan: You won't make it financially.

You: Yes, I will. I won't be rich, but God will see to it that I have enough money.

satan: You will lose custody of your children.

You: No, I won't. I won't get 100% custody, but I won't get 0%, either.

satan: Your children will turn against you forever.

You: Temporarily, maybe. But not forever. By divorcing the narc, I have a good chance to have healthy relationships with my children.

Choose a Key Bible Passage

Choose one Bible passage that speaks to you on a personal level. Focus on this passage throughout the divorce. Memorize it. Post it on your refrigerator, on the bathroom mirror, and on the dashboard of your car.

Here are some passages phone advice clients of mine have used during their divorces:

Psalm 23:4 Even though I walk through the valley of the shadow of death, I will fear no evil, for you are with me; your rod and your staff, they comfort me.

Joshua 1:9 . . . Be strong and courageous. Do not be terrified; do not be discouraged, for the Lord your God will be with you wherever you go.

Ezekiel 34:16 I will search for the lost and bring back the strays. I will bind up the injured and strengthen the weak, but the sleek and the strong I will destroy. I will shepherd the flock with justice.

Lamentations 3:22-23 Because of the Lord's great love we are not consumed, for his compassions never fail. They are new every morning; great is your faithfulness.

Matthew 11:28 "Come to me, all you who are weary and burdened, and I will give you rest."

Philippians 4:13 I can do everything through him who gives me strength.

Romans 8:37 No, in all these things we are more than conquerors through him who loved us.

CHAPTER NINE

Before You File

(In my book, *Enough is Enough*, I cover many areas of preparation before you leave and file)

There are some key actions you need to take before you file. By taking these actions, you are being what the Bible calls prudent:

The wisdom of the prudent is to give thought to their ways . . . (Proverbs 14:8)

You Need Money

Establish your own personal checking account in your name only. If you have automatic deductions or deposits, update with your new account information.

Put as much money as you can, as often as you can, into this personal checking account: income from your job, a percentage of what the narc gives you for household expenses, and contributions from family and friends and your church.

You need a war chest to pay your attorney and your bills once you leave him. When you file, most narcs will cut you off from the money they control.

Also, close joint credit cards. Get a new credit card in your name only.

Just before you file-and, ideally, just before you leave the home-take half of all savings and checking account money. Legally, you are entitled to half, and you're going to need this money.

If you don't take half, chances are good you'll never see this money again. The narc will shut you out of these accounts, spend it, move it to an account at a different bank, or give it to his family to hold for him.

Collect Financial Information

Collect-and copy-as much financial information as possible prior to leaving and filing. The narc and his nasty attorney will not turn over documents during the process. They should, but they won't. If they do turn over any documents, it will take forever and they will be incomplete. And the court won't care.

Have two copies of all financial documents-one for you and one for your attorney. Keep your copies in a safe place. Here are the documents you need:

- Tax returns for the past five years
- Bank accounts: savings, checking, business
- Retirement accounts: IRA, 401-K
- Titles to vehicles and boats
- Deeds/titles to property
- Insurance: life, home, health, disability, auto
- Mortgages and all loans
- Credit card statements for the past year

Get Your Name on Assets

The narc, unknown to you, may have only his name on key assets. Use your attorney and get your name on these assets: home, other properties, vehicles, boats . . .

Make sure your name is not the only one on major debts.

Take Photos of All Property

One day when he isn't home, take pictures-with dates on each-of every single piece of property you own. Everything. The narc may sell things or hide things as soon as he is served.

When he claims he doesn't own anything, you will have photos (dated before he was served) of all the "non-existent" property.

Narc, Financial Advisor, Attorney

If you can't secretly get the financial information, go to the narc and ask for access to it. He will probably smell a rat and realize what you are planning, but it can't be helped. Tell him: "I need to know all about our finances. What if you drop dead today?"

Do not tell him you are planning to leave and file.

If the narc refuses, which is very likely, go to your financial advisor (if you have one) privately and ask for all the information. Ask the advisor to say nothing to the narc. If he tells the narc, so be it.

If the advisor refuses to provide the information, tell him you will take legal action against him. If he still refuses, have your attorney take action.

If you don't have a financial advisor and the narc will not give you access, have your attorney take action. Legally, you are entitled to this information and you have to have it.

Email and Cell Phone

Shut down all your personal email accounts. The narc will hack into these accounts. Set up a new email account with a new password: DIrTbALL8% or LOsER!!H@

Shut down your current cell phone account and get a new account in your name only. You'll pay for it yourself. Get a burner cell phone for sensitive communications with your attorney, support team, and family.

Insurance

Work with your attorney to make sure your health, auto, life, and disability insurance remains in place and is paid for. Most narcs will cancel these policies.

Your Personal Items

Whether you leave or not, get all sentimental, irreplaceable items out of the home. Give them to family or friends. The narc will hide them, destroy them, or sell them.

Your Attorney

Be careful about communicating with your attorney. Every call, email, text, and office visit will be charged to you. Do not contact your attorney with trivial, small questions. Jot down your questions and comments for your next meeting. Keep a record of all bills and what you pay your attorney. Keep a log of all your contacts with your attorney.

Your Children

(For detailed information on preparing your children for separation and divorce, read *Enough is Enough*)

Just before you leave and file, tell your children why you are filing. Small children will tell dad, and you don't want that before you are ready.

Tell your kids the truth about dad's abuse of you. Not all the details, but the basic sketch. What he has said to you and what he has done to you. Reference specific abusive events you know they have witnessed.

Tell them dad has treated you badly and sinfully for a long time. He has hurt you terribly over and over. You will no longer tolerate his abuse. You are saving yourself and them.

Tell them your decision to leave and divorce dad is final. You will not change your mind. Tell them you believe God wants you to get a divorce.

You do not ask your children to side with you. Make it clear they can have a relationship with dad. They can spend time with dad. You will have a separate relationship with them.

Make it clear you will not speak badly about dad, but you will tell them the truth if he mistreats you or them. If he lies about you, you will correct the lies.

Tell them you will always be available, anytime, to talk with them about dad and the divorce process.

CHAPTER TEN

The Filing

Remember the 2 Timothy 3:1-5 description of a narc I shared at the beginning of chapter one? Do not forget Paul's clear action step in verse five: ". . . Have nothing to do with them."

You'll Have to File

Most narcs won't file. They don't want to lose their money or their control. They want to stay married to you and do whatever they want in their lives. They want the narrative of you filing. If a narc files, he usually has found another woman to be his narc supply.

Presenting Your Decision to Divorce

Via email, send a very brief and direct message about your decision to divorce. Give no explanation for why. None.

Any explanation is a sign of weakness and will prompt the narc to try to suck you into endless discussions about your decision. Giving no explanation-ever-empowers you and gives him nothing to specifically refute.

As I have instructed you, you will tell your children why. If they tell the narc your reasons for filing, that's fine. When he brings up what you have told the children, ignore him.

If you're not able to physically separate, here is your email to the narc:

After a great deal of thought and prayer, I have decided to divorce you. That decision is final and I will not discuss it. I would prefer this process to be amicable, and of course we will work out the time we each spend with the children. I wish you the best in your ongoing life. We will live for the time being in the same home, coparenting and maintaining the household. I will only communicate with you via this email address (give it) and only about necessary issues: time with the children, money issues, household chores, and emergencies.

If you are able to physically separate, you'll send your email after you leave. Your email will be the same as the one above, with one exception. Omit this line: We will live for the time being in the same home, coparenting and maintaining the household.

If you're forced to live with the narc during the divorce, only communicate via email. I don't care if the narc is standing two feet away from you-only use email. Or, an app your attorney sets up.

Serving the Narc

Serve the narc the divorce papers as soon as possible after sending your email message. If you are living with him, send the email when he's gone for a few days. Or, take the kids with you for a few days on a trip and send the email while you're gone.

This will give the narc a chance to process it and start his adjustment. And, you can avoid the initial outrage and "how could you" reactions.

Don't serve him at his work. There's no need to further inflame him. He can be served at home or through the mail. Your attorney will advise you.

The "date of separation" is important. Make this date as close to the filing as possible. You can use the date you file. All your community property is to be split from the date of separation. He can empty his bank account and buy expensive items, and you will not lose your half of that money. Any debts he runs up after the date of separation will not be yours.

Communication After Filing

Once you have sent your email and he has been served, only communicate with him via email and only about the necessary issues I previously mentioned.

Do not, do not, do not communicate with him about the divorce. Do not, do not, do not communicate with him about the marriage. Do not, do not, do not communicate with him about any personal matters.

The narc is a roommate and a coparent and a business associate and nothing more. Well, he is a dirtball, too.

Any communication about the divorce, the marriage, and personal matters will embolden him, weaken you, and give him hope and lead to more attempts to dialogue.

Express no sympathy for him. He'll get plenty of that from the Peanut Gallery. Do not disagree with him. Give him zero response. Give him nothing back.

The only time you will-briefly and directly-respond to him is when he attacks you or lies about you in front of your children. More on this in the Personal War section.

Give Him the Brick Wall

The narc will do everything in his power to get you to engage, to interact, to respond to him about the divorce. He wants to:

- Change your mind
- Upset you
- Know what you are thinking and feeling
- Keep you off balance
- Make you doubt your decision
- Make you defend your decision
- Make you suffer for your decision
- Weaken your resolve
- Regain control over you

He'll ignore your boundary to only communicate via email. As you know, the narc has never respected your boundaries. Why should he start now?

He'll want to meet with you to talk-No Response

He'll want to take you out to dinner-No Response

He'll want to sit with you in church-No Response

He'll want to sit with you at the kid's activities-No Response

He'll want to facetime-No Response

He'll want to talk on the phone-No Response

He'll want to text, to use Facebook messages-No Response

He'll want to communicate through cards and letters-No Response

Do not respond to the narc unless it is about a necessary issue. Give him nothing. Nothing but a silent brick wall.

You will have plenty of internal responses and emotions to his efforts to engage you. Share these, vent these with your support team warriors. Never with the narc.

Classic Narc Reactions to Filing

I've covered these narc reactions in earlier chapters, but here is a brief summary to refresh your memory:

- Begging, pleading, promising to change
- Getting the Peanut Gallery to pressure you

- Pretending it's okay, let's be amicable, let's do a collaborative divorce, I'll be fair in the settlement
- Lovebombing on an epic scale
- Repenting on an epic-though fake-scale
- Complaining that you are not responding to all his incredible changes
- Mentioning your unforgiveness
- Adopting the role of Bible scholar and telling you that you have no biblical reason to divorce him
- Trying to make you feel guilty for divorcing him
- Adopting the role of Parenting expert and telling you that the divorce will seriously harm the children
- Becoming angry and raging at you
- Cutting you off with the silent treatment (let's hope he does this because it will give you a break)

What do you do in response to all these narc reactions? (and this isn't a complete list) You know the answer to this pop quiz. Nothing. You do nothing. You ignore every effort by the narc to get you to respond.

Don't Waver

I did a whole chapter on this topic. (chapter two) But many things are worth repeating, especially for a person going through the traumatic process of divorcing a narc.

Do not waver. Do. Not. Waver. Stay on course with the divorce, no matter what the narc throws at you.

CHAPTER ELEVEN

The Personal War: Mistakes to Avoid

If you don't waver in the face of the narc's lovebombing, repenting, siccing the Peanut Gallery on you, and all his attempts to get you to stop the divorce, he'll get nasty and go into attack mode.

He'll go to open warfare against you in three main areas:

- Personal
- Parental
- Legal

I'll cover the Personal War first.

Guard Yourself

Above all else, guard your heart, for it is the wellspring of life. (Proverbs 4:23)

The narc is coming after your heart. He's always beaten on your heart. Now, he'll go nuclear.

One of my YouTube subscribers said it best: "For the narc, it's control or destroy."

Here are key mistakes to avoid in the Personal War. If you haven't made these mistakes yet, don't make them. If you have, that's okay. Most persons who divorce a narc make these mistakes.

Just stop making them.

Don't Try to Understand the narc

Stop all your efforts to figure out why the narc acts the way he does. Who cares? Even if you could figure him out (which you can't), it wouldn't make any difference. He won't change anyway.

You do not have the time and energy to waste on a fruitless quest to understand what makes the narc tick. You are dropping your codependency, remember?

Don't Believe You are a narcissist

Just about every narc being divorced will accuse his spouse of being a narc. He will build an entire, elaborate case for your narcissism.

Do not entertain this ridiculous, false charge.

Here are three ways to know you are not a narc.

First, if you wonder if you are a narc, you aren't a narc. narcs never wonder this.

Second, if you struggle with guilt over your sins, you aren't a narc. narcs don't ever feel guilt.

Third, if you genuinely apologize, feel badly for the pain you have caused others, and actually change your behavior, you aren't a narc. narcs don't do genuine apologies, have zero empathy, and don't change their behavior for more than a few months. (if that long)

Don't Be Weak and Nice

You are used to humoring the narc. Placating him. Taking care of him. Being concerned about his feelings. Giving him control and power so that he will be happy and not abuse you. Taking all the blame. Believing his lies.

You're such a nice person that you will probably question your decision to divorce him. Listen to me, nice person. You have made the right decision. His post-filing, vicious personal attacks will confirm your decision.

There is no room for niceness toward the narc in this divorce war. Don't think that being nice to the narc will make him be nice to you. That is codependent thinking.

Being nice to him weakens you. It is enabling behavior. Nice will give him power and lead to even more attacks on you.

It's okay to *fake* strong and assertive until you can actually *be* strong and assertive. As you heal and gain confidence, you will become a strong and assertive person.

One way to project strength is to not respond-ever-to his personal attacks. Silence communicates strength. Your silence will drive him nuts, which is what he deserves.

Don't Let Fools Make You Feel Guilty

I covered this in chapter five, in the Peanut Gallery discussion.

Give these misguided fools no time and energy. Do not attempt to persuade them. Ignore them.

Don't Believe the Divorce Will Destroy You

Read this list of perfectly normal stress reactions everyone who divorces a narc experiences:

- Heart palpitations
- Racing heart
- Stomach problems
- Migraines
- Brain fog
- Memory issues
- Trouble concentrating
- Physical exhaustion
- Depression
- Anxiety
- Panic attacks
- Much lower tolerance level
- Crying jags
- Anger outbursts
- PTSD symptoms
- Eating less
- Eating more
- Sleeping less
- Sleeping more
- Often feeling overwhelmed
- Feeling distant from God

All. Perfectly. Normal. You will survive the divorce and all these stress reactions will go away.

The divorce process will not destroy you. What will destroy you is staying married to the narc.

Don't Play the Should Have Game

It's very easy -and quite common-to play The Should Have Game.

- I should have seen the red flags during dating
- I should have never married the narc
- I should have kept my job
- I should have told my family the truth right away
- I should have spoken up and protected my kids
- I should have divorced him years ago

Leave these regrets behind. You are taking action now. You can work through your regrets later. Now is not the time.

Warriors don't take time to dwell on past regrets and poor decisions. That's a distraction they can't afford. They fight hard in the present.

If someone breaks into your home, you don't waste time regretting that you didn't lock the door. You fight to protect yourself and your children.

Don't Shield Your Children From the Truth

You have "protected" your children from the truth about their father long enough. It was never a good idea to hold back the truth from them. This is a war for your children's hearts and minds. If you don't fight the war by telling your children the truth about the narc's personal attacks, you'll lose them.

Older children (ten and up) can know the details of dad's attacks on you. Show them his nasty texts, emails, and voicemails. You won't show them every single false, vicious communication, but you need to show them enough so they understand dad's sinful behavior.

Younger children (under ten) can know general information about dad's attacks and abuse during the divorce. "Dad called me a nasty name today." "Dad sent me ten texts today saying I am a liar and have no right to divorce him." "Dad accused me today of not being a good Christian."

As I mentioned in an earlier chapter, you will tell your children (whatever their ages) every lie the narc tells about you and you will correct these lies.

CHAPTER TWELVE

The Personal War: What You Can Do

The narc's relentless personal attacks will have an impact on you. What you need to do is take steps to reduce the impact and manage your emotions.

Your Emotions

As the narc bombards you with his attacks, you will be (at times):

- Depressed
- Sad
- Wounded
- Anxious
- Fearful
- Overwhelmed
- Stressed

All these emotional reactions are normal. Everyone who divorces a narc experiences them.

Do not share any of your emotions with the narc. Ever. It will thrill his evil heart to know he's getting to you.

Do not share any of your emotions with the Peanut Gallery of fools. They couldn't care less about your pain. They will tell you all your pain is your fault, because you filed divorce.

Do not share any of your emotions with *his* family. It doesn't matter if you have been close to any of his people. Blood goes with blood. They will side with the narc. And, they will act as spies for him. Cut them off.

Do not share any of your deep emotions with your children. They can't handle their emotions and yours. Plus, they may tell the narc about your pain and you don't want that. They will see some emotion from you because of his attacks, of course. Just work to mute your emotions around them.

Vent your emotions fully with God and the key members of your support team.

Communication With the narc

Use one form of digital communication with the narc. Not in person. Not on the phone. Consider using a parenting app that records everything. Your attorney will know which app to recommend.

Read these communication strategies from spouses who divorced a narc:

- "In my responses to him, I only responded when necessary and used the fewest words possible. I tried to stick to yes or no."
- "My response was consistent no matter what ugly things he said. Ignore, ignore, ignore. Refuse to take the bait."
- "I was more at peace when I let his infuriating, crazy-making comments go. I focused only on the specific issue at hand."
- "I was calm in his presence and in all communications, no matter how he acted."
- "When he sent me a message, I would-if it wasn't an emergency-not respond right away. This gave me more control."

Refute the narc's Lies

You will refute and correct the narc's lies about you *only* to these persons below.

Your Children

When the narc attacks you/lies about you in front of the children, you must respond verbally asap every time. You will no longer allow criticism, threats, lies, yelling, and cursing to pass without a firm and honest response.

These responses have nothing to do with changing the narc's behavior. He will be a dirtball narc until the day he dies. Your responses empower you, build respect from your children, show your kids the truth about dad, and protect your relationship with them.

Tell your kids to expect dad to lie about you. Ask them to always come to you when they feel uneasy about something he's said about you.

Use brief, assertive, one-way comments to his public attacks. One-way means you make the statement and move on. You don't get into a back and forth with the idiot narc.

You can use these responses:

- "That's a lie"
- "That's disrespectful"
- "You are sinning"
- "That is mean"
- "You are way out of line"

When you find out the narc has made an attack on you to the children when you were not present, you will say nothing to the narc. You go the child asap and correct the lie. Every time.

You don't make an attack on the narc. You simply tell the child the truth:

- "What dad said is vicious and untrue"
- "What dad said is a lie"
- "Dad is trying to turn you against me"
- "I have not had an affair"
- "I am not mentally unstable"
- "Dad is trying to hurt me because I am divorcing him"

Your Boss

The narc would love to cause problems for you at work. He'd love to get you demoted or fired. So, tell your boss to expect to hear false charges about you from the narc.

When the narc makes bogus allegations about you, tell your boss the truth. And ask your boss to not respond to the narc. Check with your attorney-these false allegations may be used as leverage.

Those in the Legal Circus (I mean System)

The narc will lie about you to everyone involved in your case: the judge, the Guardian Ad

Litem, the social worker, any counselor you have seen, the psychologist who does the psychological evaluations of you and the narc and the kids, your children's teachers, your children's coaches . . .

Since these persons have a say in the custody decision, you will calmly and firmly deny the narc's lies and speak the truth.

Righteous Anger is Your Friend

The divorce process is not the time to work through your trauma and forgive the narc. That will come after the divorce is final and the dust has settled. You can't do this difficult work and get through the divorce at the same time.

Now is the time for righteous anger. God gets angry (Malachi 2:13-16). Jesus gets angry (Matthew 23:1-36). David gets angry (Psalm 69:24-25). Abigail gets angry at her narc husband (1 Samuel 25:25). Paul gets angry (Galatians 2:11).

In Ecclesiastes 3:8, we read:

A time to love and a time to hate, a time for war and a time for peace.

Not many Christian psychologists will tell you this, but I am telling you: This is a time to hate. This is a time for war.

Look at these benefits of righteous anger:

- Power to cope
- Clarity that cuts through your brain fog
- Confidence
- Strength
- Self-esteem
- Self-respect
- Energy and motivation to fight
- Toughness
- Endurance
- Reduction of your anxiety and depression

Also, righteous anger protects your relationship with your children. It will help you maintain their respect and trust. If you are weak and pitiful, your kids won't feel secure with you. They'll get closer to the narc. They'll believe his lies about you and side with him.

Righteous anger is the one emotion you do want your kids to see. It shows them a woman who is furious and will not passively tolerate another second of the narc's abuse. If the kids report your anger to the narc, fine. It will send him a message of strength and resolve.

For a full explanation of how to get righteously angry and stay righteously angry, read my book: *My Spouse Wants Out.*

Find Other Abused Spouses

It is empowering and encouraging to spend time-online or in person-with other persons who have a narc in their lives.

These persons could be already divorced or currently in a divorce. They will understand what you are going through with the narc.

They'll pray with you, give you Scripture, support you, listen to you vent, laugh with you, join you in mocking the narc, and give you practical ideas on how to navigate through the divorce.

They will help you and you will help them.

Ask your pastor (if he is totally supportive of you) for names. You may find these persons at a Celebrate Recovery or DivorceCare group, a local domestic violence center, or a local women's center.

Two excellent online groups are run by Leslie Vernick and Shelley Martinkus. Google them.

Protect Yourself

It is unlikely the narc will attack you physically (unless he's been violent with you before), but unlikely doesn't help you if he does. The loss of control and money can send a narc over the edge.

Be prepared for violence. Stay alert at all times. Buy a gun. Or, buy a Hero gun or Aiiro, which fire chemical irritants. Or, buy pepper spray.

CHAPTER THIRTEEN

The Personal War: What the narc Will Do

As you deal with the personal attacks I'm about to describe, keep this verse in mind:

His speech is smooth as butter, yet war is in his heart; his words are more soothing than oil, yet they are drawn swords. (Psalm 55:21)

The narc is charming and persuasive to the outside world, but vicious and evil to you. He is going to war against you.

A Shift in Attack

The narc knows now you will not stop the divorce. So, he will shift his attack campaign. Now, he wants to:

- Make everyone turn against you
- Make your kids turn against you
- Make himself look like the victim
- Make you suffer so much that you'll quit and he wins in the settlement

The narc Hijacks Your Pain

Your decision to file divorce is exhibit A in the narc's case to put you in the abuser/perpetrator role. He will hijack your pain-the pain *he* caused-and take it all for himself.

He is shocked-shocked, I tell you-that you filed. And now even more shocked because you will not applaud his changes and cancel the divorce. There must be something seriously wrong with you.

You are no longer the victim of his abuse. Oh, no! *He* is now the victim of your abuse.

Here is what he'll communicate-to you and anyone else who will listen-to prove his victimhood. I have included responses that you can express to God and key support team members (not to the narc).

narc: I never saw this coming.

You (capital Y): I told you a million times about my misery and my needs.

narc: I wasn't that bad of a husband.

You: Actually, much, much worse than bad. Abusive. That's why I'm divorcing you.

narc: I was never good enough for you.

You: That's true. Because you never tried.

narc: I did make some mistakes, but that's in the past.

You: Some? Try too many to count. Mistakes? Wrong word. Try abusive, destructive, evil behaviors. In the past? You've never stopped abusing me. You're still at it.

narc: You won't forgive me.

You: Yes, I will, all in due time. First, I'll divorce you, so I can heal and forgive you.

narc: I am a godly man now.

You: (once your laughing fit is over) No, you are a man pretending to be a godly man. I hope you do become a godly man, for your sake and for the sake of our kids.

Opposite World

Just as the narc did in your marriage, he will play the opposite world game in your divorce. He will accuse you of all the things *he* is guilty of doing.

One TikTok subscriber put it this way: "A narc's accusations are his confessions." Absolutely true. But, nobody except you and your team of warriors know this truth.

Get ready for these opposite world gems:

- I'm not a narcissist, you are
- I'm not abusive, you are
- I'm not ungodly, you are
- I didn't destroy our marriage, you did
- I'm not a liar, you are
- I'm not a spender, you are
- I'm not unloving, you are
- I'm not a bad parent, you are
- I'm not mean to the dog, you are

The narc will have specific-and bogus- examples to back up each one of these accusations. Good thing you won't be reading them or responding to them.

Everything is Used Against You

You know how scientists take one chipped tooth and create an entire dinosaur? The narc will take anything from your past and use it to create a profile of a crazy, unstable, and messed up person. He knows personal, private things about you and he'll use them against you:

- Your dysfunctional family
- Your conflicts with your parents and siblings

- Your conflicts with friends
- Any jobs you've lost or left
- Any alcohol or drug use (even if years ago)
- Your previous romantic relationships, including marriages
- Your struggles with anxiety and depression or any emotional issue
- Any counseling you have had
- The medication you've taken for emotional issues
- Any abortions you've had
- Any sexual abuse you have suffered
- Negative things you've said about others

Attacks on Your Personality

He'll use your personality traits against you. Normal traits are turned into huge negatives:

- Outgoing and friendly . . . you are a flirt who craves the attention of all members of the opposite sex
- Assertive and confident . . . you are controlling
- Quiet . . . you are boring and won't open up
- Not affectionate . . . you hate sex and are frigid

- Type A . . . a workaholic who neglects him and the kids
- Creative . . . an irresponsible flake
- Messy . . . an absolute slob and hoarder who forces the forces the family to live in filth

A Cascade of Accusations

In his massive smear campaign, he'll tell you and others that you are:

- Emotionally unstable
- Crazy
- Mentally ill
- Suicidal
- Irrational
- Bipolar
- A rageaholic
- Violent
- Homicidal (you have threatened his life)
- A liar
- An abuser
- A narcissist
- A hypocrite
- A bad mother
- An unfit mother
- An awful Christian

- Not a Christian at all
- A man hater (actually, you just hate him)
- An adulteress (you have had multiple affairs)
- Bisexual
- A lesbian (it's the only explanation for you not wanting him to touch you)
- A drug addict
- An alcoholic
- A borderline

Basically, he'll describe you as the worst person who ever walked the face of the earth.

Threats

The narc will throw threat after threat at you. He will certainly try to make good on these threats, so take these seriously:

- I will leave you with no money
- I'll drag the divorce out as long as I can
- I'll get full custody of the kids
- I'll turn the kids against you
- I'll get a protective order so you can't see the kids

- I'll get your family and friends to turn on you
- I'll turn everyone you know against you
- I'll get our pastor to do church discipline on you
- I'll expose all your secrets
- I'll get you fired from your job
- I'll get full custody of the dog
- I'll never stop making your life a living Hell
- I'll find a new woman and the kids will love her

You already know to give him no response to his attacks, accusations, and threats. But, document each one-keep copies of emails and texts if he is stupid and arrogant enough to send them to you in these forms-and give them to your attorney.

CHAPTER FOURTEEN

The Parental War: Mistakes to Avoid

In this war, the persons you are most concerned about are your precious children. No one else even comes close.

- You want to protect them from the worst parts of the divorce nightmare
- You want to protect them from the narc
- You want to protect your relationship with them

God wants these same things for you and your children. These chapters on the Parental War are designed to help you do your best to protect your children.

The narc will throw your children into the middle of the war. And try to keep them there. Because that's what narcs do.

Don't Minimize the Trauma for Your Kids

For your kids, the divorce is traumatic. There's no getting around that awful truth. The divorce is necessary, but traumatic.

They won't understand your decision to divorce. They have seen you tolerate the abuse for so long that they don't see his behavior as abusive. It's normal for them.

They will think, "Why are you divorcing dad now? What's changed? This makes no sense. Your selfish decision is disrupting my life!"

They will feel massive pain and the narc will convince them *you* are causing their pain with the divorce.

They don't understand the terrible pain dad has put you through for years. They don't understand the damage he's done to *them* over the years. They have learned-largely from you-how to cope and adjust to his behavior and do not see it as abusive.

He's just dad. They love him. They don't understand narcissism. They don't see him as a monster.

In time, there's a good chance they'll understand what dad is really like. (if you don't divorce him, they never will, just so you know) They'll understand your decision to divorce him. They'll understand you acted to save yourself and them.

But, they won't fully grasp these truths until well after the divorce is final.

Don't Think the narc is a Good Father

Many of my phone advice clients tell me: "He's awful to me, but he's a good father." After throwing up in the bucket I keep by my desk, I tell them: "No, he's not. He's a terrible father. His abuse of you hurts the kids. Modeling abusive words and behaviors hurts the kids. Undermining your authority as a parent hurts the kids. Trying to turn the kids against you-which he has been doing for years-hurts the kids. Don't tell me he's a good father. He's a bad, abusive father."

Thinking he is a good father and, worse, expressing that to the kids, weakens your position. If he is such a good father, the kids will wonder-and rightfully so-why you are divorcing him? Why are you giving them less time with their wonderful father?

You will not tell the kids directly that he is a terrible father. You will, by telling them the truth about dad, show them over time this difficult truth.

Don't Think the narc Loves the Kids

He'll say to anyone who will listen how much he loves his kids. He'll repeat this statement many, many times during the divorce. It makes people think he's a great father, a great person, and that you are an awful person for reducing his time with the kids. No one-except for your support team-will believe you are trying to save the kids.

This "I love my kids" mantra is a lie from the pit of Hell. The narc only loves himself. There is no room for the kids or anyone else in his selfish heart.

If any of your kids, no matter how old they are, realize the truth about dad and tell him the truth about his abuse, they will see just how much he loves them. He will turn on them like a rabid dog. He will reject them. He will cut them off.

The kids are his property. He wants to control them. He wants their attention, their adulation, their worship. He demands complete loyalty, which means they love him and hate you. He wants them to make him look good. He wants to use them to destroy you.

He couldn't care less about the kids. He doesn't care what happens to them. What they do with their lives. If they succeed, he'll take the credit. If they fail, he'll just blame you: "It was their mother's decision to divorce me that messed them up."

Don't Keep the Kids Out of Counseling

Do whatever it takes to keep your kids in counseling during the divorce. Beg, borrow and beg and borrow some more to pay the counselor.

Find a Christian, licensed, experienced counselor who understands narcissism and has helped other children get through a divorce. Because the narc will insist on being involved, your counselor needs to know how to handle him.

Your counselor will help your kids:

- Understand why you are divorcing their father
- Deal with the loss of the marriage and family
- Deal with the narc's attempts to alienate them from you

- Avoid destructive behaviors and develop healthy coping skills
- Maintain a healthy relationship with you

Don't Hold Back the Truth

Read what one of my YouTube subscribers wrote me: "I followed my counselor's advice to not tell my children what their father was really like. I protected him during the marriage and during the divorce. Now, I have a very strained relationship with my kids. They don't trust me."

I told this mom to fire this counselor immediately and get a new one. I also told her to read my book, *I Didn't Want a Divorce, Now What?* because it would help her heal her relationship with her kids.

Don't make this mom's mistake. Do your research and choose the right counselor. Check out the counselor's website, get recommendations from persons you trust, and meet with her individually first to make sure she is the right one.

I have already told you this, and I'm going to tell you again: Tell your kids the truth about the narc before, during, and after the divorce.

The narc is constantly pushing his anti-you narrative with the kids. You have to counter that narrative with the truth.

The narc lies to the kids *all the time.* He's been lying to them for years. He won't ever stop. When you don't speak truth to them, they will believe his lies.

Your kids need a steady diet of truth from you.

Don't Think the narc Won't Alienate the Kids

The narc doesn't just want the children to prefer him over you. Oh, no. He wants far more than that.

The narc wants the kids to blame you for all the marital problems. He wants the kids to blame you for the divorce. He wants them to hate you. To disobey you. To cut you off and have no relationship with you.

If that isn't evil, I don't know what is.

He will rejoice as he turns your own children against you. He's been working to alienate them from you for years. Now, he will ramp up that operation.

If he can alienate your kids, you will suffer deeply and that's what he wants. Also, many people will believe you are the problem. You are the bad guy. You are the narcissist. You are the abuser.

All he has to do is say: "Her own kids hate her and they love me." It follows that you are to blame for everything.

Never Underestimate the Evil of the narc

The Bible describes a narc this way:

. . . who delight in doing wrong and rejoice in the perverseness of evil . . . (Proverbs 2:14)

He doesn't just do wrong. He *delights* in doing wrong. He doesn't just do evil things. He *rejoices* in his evil behavior.

One of my phone clients emailed me: "He told me that he would make my life a living Hell until my daughter turned eighteen, and that is the only promise he kept."

CHAPTER FIFTEEN

The Parental War: What You Can Do

The narc knows that the one way he can hurt you the most is through your children. He has no concern for their welfare. He will use them to damage you. He will hurt them to hurt you.

You must be wise to protect your children. I want to help you apply this verse:

. . . for wisdom is more precious than rubies, and nothing you desire can compare with her. (Proverbs 8:11)

Here are some practical, wise ways to protect your kids in the divorce.

Expect at Least One Child to Be Won Over

The narc has been alienating the kids for years. Undermining your authority. Breaking down their trust in you. Chipping away at their respect for you. Lying about you.

The narc has to be in total control of the kids. And, he has to have their undivided loyalty and love.

The narc has built in advantages in the war for your children's hearts. He is dad and they love dad. They want his love and approval. Plus, the narc is a superb liar. He'll fool them just like he fooled you. At least, for a while.

Here's a brutal truth you will hate me for bringing up: It's very likely the narc will turn at least one of your kids against you. I've seen this happen many, many times.

By following the teaching in these three Parental War chapters (fourteen, fifteen, and sixteen), there's a good chance your kids will figure out the truth and come back to you.

Get a Custody Agreement Asap

Have your attorney work out a timesharing plan as soon as possible. This temporary plan will be in place until the custody agreement is finalized in the divorce settlement.

It may have to be a fifty-fifty time split. Get ready for that. Most states are doing this arrangement. (the only good news about this is that, after the divorce, very few narcs will spend 50 % of the time with the kids)

Without this temporary plan, the narc will have a field day. He'll call and text the kids whenever he wants. He'll pick them up and drop them off whenever he wants. He'll love causing chaos in your life.

Through your attorney and the court, establish a detailed and specific timesharing plan:

- The days and times he contacts the kids and how he does it: phone, text, email, special app
- How long he talks/communicates with each child
- The days and times he is with the kids
- When he picks them up and when he drops them off
- When he will have them on special days: their birthdays, holidays, vacations . . .

It will take time for your attorney to get a deal in place. The narc will be in no hurry to make a deal. In the meantime, work with your attorney and come up with a reasonable timesharing plan. Have your attorney present it to the narc. If he won't follow it, you do your best to follow it.

Expect the narc to ignore your timesharing plan. He knows he doesn't have to abide by it, so he won't. Bite the bullet and ride out this boundary breaking phase. Let the kids know the plan and tell them every time dad breaks it. When he disregards the plan, make very brief, no emotion comments to him. Not to change his behavior, but to maintain your voice and show the kids your assertiveness.

Once you have a court-ordered plan in place, stick to the plan rigidly. Make no exceptions-ever-unless there is a true emergency. If you give the narc an inch, he'll take ten miles.

Document each time the narc breaks the deal. And he will break the deal. Because narcs do whatever they want to do.

Prepare Your Children

You need to get your kids ready for what the narc will say and do in the divorce.

He'll Lie

Let them know the narc will lie to them and tell them the lies they are likely to hear:

- "Your mother is having an affair"

- "Your mother is a lesbian"
- "Your mother is crazy"
- "Your mother is bipolar"
- "Your mother is trying to turn you against me"
- "Your mother told me she doesn't love you"
- "Your mother is way too strict because she is mean and doesn't trust you"
- "Your mother is a narcissist"
- "Your mother won't forgive me"
- "Your mother destroyed our marriage"
- "Your mother doesn't care about your pain"

Tell your kids: "Every time dad says something and you wonder if it's true, come to me and I will tell you the truth. I'll never tell dad what we talk about."

He'll Make You Choose

Warn your kids that the narc will force them to choose between him and you. He will try to make them hate you and cut you off.

Tell your kids: "If you don't fully support him, be ready for him to reject you. You don't have to choose him or me. You can have a relationship with each of us. You don't have to take sides. I want you to have a relationship with your dad if you want to. It's okay to pretend to dad that you choose him, just to get him off your back."

If an older child (12 and up) does side with you and doesn't want to have contact with the narc, fully support that child's decision. Make it clear you did nothing to influence the decision. (though you are secretly thrilled) Working with your attorney, do all you can to limit that child's contact with the narc.

He'll Give You Total Freedom

Let them know the narc, in order to win them over, will let them do whatever they want in his home.

Tell your kids: "Be careful with all the freedom dad is going to give you. I hope and pray you follow God's standards when you are with dad. I will enforce God's standards in my home because I believe God's way is best for you."

For a thorough, detailed manual on training your kids to manage the narc parent, get my wonderful friend Laurel Slade-Waggoner's book: *Don't Let Their Crazy Make Your Kids Crazy.*

God's Standards in Your Home

Following the Bible's teaching, establish clear behavior standards in your home. Let your kids know-both verbally and in writing-how you expect them to act when they are with you.

If they choose to obey, they will be rewarded. If they choose to disobey, they will receive consequences.

You will cover:

- Phone time
- All screen time
- What they can view and when they can view it and for how long they can view it
- The music they can listen to
- Grades
- Homework
- Chores
- Their respect for you
- Church attendance
- No alcohol or drugs or sex

Someone has to be the parent. The narc certainly won't be, so it will have to be you. For my complete guide to raising kids of all ages, get my Focus on the Family published book: *Parenting is Hard and Then You Die.*

God's Way and the narc's Way

Follow Deuteronomy 6:4-9 and teach your children that obeying the Bible is the best way to live. Show them, with brief comments, that the narc's way is wrong and God's way is right.

- "Dad lied about me. The Bible says, don't lie."
- "Dad cursed. The Bible says, don't use coarse talk and don't use the Lord's name in vain."
- "Dad chooses to not go to church. The Bible says, we are to be in church."
- "Dad has a girlfriend. The Bible says, this is the sin of adultery."
- "Dad says I have no biblical reason to divorce him. The Bible says, yes I do."

Read the kids the Bible passages that show dad is sinning and what God says.

You don't lecture. You don't rant and rave about the narc's sin. You don't tear down the narc and his character, tempting though that is.

You simply and briefly point out the narc's way and God's way.

No Family Time

Whether you are physically separated or not, do not spend any time together as a family. Do everything separately. You will have time with the kids and the narc will have time with the kids.

Meals and TV watching-as much as possible-are separate. Church is separate. Birthdays are separate. Holidays are separate. The kid's activities and sports are separate. You will not sit with him or be with him anywhere.

You are preparing your kids for divorce, where everything will be separate. Your kids may beg you to include dad. Give them a firm no. Tell them: "I'm divorcing him because he has abused me for years and I don't want to be around him."

Spending time as a family:

- Is awkward and painful for you
- Confuses the kids
- Gives the narc a chance to look good
- Gives the narc a chance to attack you

- Does not get the kids ready for life after the divorce

Do Not Quit

Do not quit and give him too much in the divorce settlement. This isn't just because you get shafted and it makes you struggle financially. Your kids will see your capitulation as an admission of guilt. They will lose respect for you.

Your kids need to see you fighting to the bitter end. It's not about winning or losing. You may very well lose legally. It's about showing them that standing up for what is right and fair is important.

If you lose in the legal arena, so be it. At least you went down fighting for justice. Even if you lose legally, you win in the eyes of your children.

And, keep in mind that fighting to the end prepares you for your post-divorce life. The narc will continue to attack you and you need to be battle-hardened. If you show weakness and quit in the divorce, the narc will attack you all the more after the divorce.

CHAPTER SIXTEEN

The Parental War: What the narc Will Do

In the divorce, the narc will live out these words of Jesus:

"For out of the heart come evil thoughts, murder, adultery, sexual immorality, theft, false testimony, slander." (Matthew 15:19)

Most narcs will be guilty of all these sins, except murder, in the divorce. And, of course, your kids will be impacted by these sins.

The narc Will Weaponize the Kids

The narc will not be a parent to the kids. He doesn't care about them or their welfare. He'll say he does, but he doesn't. They exist to please him. They exist to make him look good and make you look bad.

He wants no conflict with them. He wants to be their friend. He wants their sympathy. He wants their adulation. He wants their complete support.

He wants to win over their hearts and minds. He wants to turn them against you. He wants to use them to humiliate you, damage you, make you suffer for filing, and keep more of his money.

Here is what the narc will do to damage you through the kids.

The Fun, Fun, Fun Dad

The narc will spoil the kids beyond belief by giving them:

- Money
- Gifts
- Toys
- A car
- A new phone
- A video game system
- New clothes
- Jewelry
- Trips to fun locations
- Tattoos

Mr. Freedom

He will also use a very effective technique called freedom. He'll allow them to:

- Spend as much time as they want on their screens
- Watch whatever they want on their screens

- Do whatever they want on social media
- Hang out with low quality, questionable friends
- Stay up late and get up late
- Miss school
- Not do homework
- Not do chores
- Eat whatever they want
- Decide to be homosexual, lesbian, bisexual, or transgender
- Drink alcohol and do drugs

Whether you are separated or not, the narc will spoil the kids. If you have adult children who are living on their own, he'll shower them and their kids with money and gifts. And, if he has his own business, he'll offer them jobs. He'll make it clear that, in return for their support, he'll continue to be financially generous.

He'll tell your minor kids, "I trust you. Your mother doesn't." He doesn't care if the gifts and freedom hurt them. Whatever. If the kids act out, it's your fault because you filed and disrupted their lives.

Tell the kids: "I know it's more fun at dad's home. I get that. But that much freedom isn't good for you. It's not real life. In real life, you don't get everything you want. In my home, we will have fun within limits. You can earn rewards and freedom by following God's standards. I believe this is what is best for you."

If a teenager, thirteen and up, wants to spend more time with the narc, let it happen. It you fight it, you'll lose and the narc will use your resistance against you. Your child will hate you and blame you. Like the father in Luke 15:11-32, let your prodigal child go.

With your attorney's guidance, document the narc's irresponsible behavior that compromises the welfare of your children. Say nothing to the narc, but document. If you can prove he's harming the kids, you may be able to use this information in the legal process.

The Boundary Breaker

The narc will routinely break the timesharing plan-the temporary one and the one the court orders. He's selfish and wants to do things his way. He also wants to cause you inconvenience and pain.

When the narc calls late for his scheduled time to talk with the kids, inform him that he missed the window. He'll have a fit, but you're not listening. If the deal is he calls at 7:30 to talk for fifteen minutes, when he calls after 7:45, he doesn't get to talk to them. When he calls late but before 7:45, he only gets to talk until 7:45.

When he is late to pick up the kids, have no reaction. Don't text to find out where he is. That's what he wants. You don't care if he comes late. If you have plans, go to your backup plan.

When he cancels his time with the kids at the last second or doesn't show up, have no reaction. Don't text to find out what happened. If you have plans, go to your backup plan. Tell the kids: "I guess dad had something else he wanted to do."

When he keeps the kids much longer than the agreed upon deal, show no emotion. Simply text him: "Let me know when you'll return them." And, give consequences: "You'll be responsible for their homework and for them missing their activities."

If there is a court order specifying how long he can have the kids, call the police and show them the order. The police will have to enforce it. He'll have a fit, but you're not listening.

Document every time the narc violates your timesharing agreement.

The Interrogator

The narc will bombard the kids with questions about you. He wants to know:

- What you do
- Who you spend time with
- What members of the opposite sex you spend time with
- How you are feeling about him and the divorce
- Who you talk to and what you talk about
- What you spend money on
- What you say about him
- What your reactions are to his behavior
- What you and your attorney are up to
- What outings, trips, and vacations you are planning

He'll try to make your kids spies. He wants information so he knows how to attack you.

Teach your children how to avoid answering his questions. Tell them to give these responses to him:

- "I don't know" (kids say this a lot, anyway)

- "I don't want to talk about mom"
- "Mom doesn't tell me anything"
- "These questions make me uncomfortable"
- "Why don't you ask her?"
- "Let's talk about you and what you're doing" (narcs love to talk about themselves)

Warn them that dad will get angry when they don't tell him what he wants to know.

Don't share personal information, your emotions (other than anger), or any legal strategies with your children. They don't need to know and they may tell the narc.

Let your kids see you happy and enjoying life with them. Say nothing about the narc. Ask them no questions about him. You only talk about him to correct his lies and make brief comments on his sinful behavior.

The Thief

The narc won't give you a dime, not even for the kids and their needs. Guess what? The court doesn't care. Eventually, the court will order him to pay you a set amount. But that will take months. Months!

Once he's ordered to pay you, he still won't. He'll refuse. He'll stall. He'll cry poor. He'll pay late. He'll give you less than the ordered amount. Guess what? The court doesn't care.

This is why, before you file, it's vital to take half the money, have a war chest, get a job, and have money coming in.

Tell the kids the truth: "Dad is choosing to not give me money to take care of you. We will have to live very simply." Say nothing to the narc.

The Adulterer

The narc may very well hook up with another woman during the divorce process. After all, he has needs. Since he has no conscience, he'll see nothing wrong with this relationship. He believes you two are already divorced. It's your fault, anyway.

He will expose your kids to this skank. That's right, skank. What kind of person dates (and has sex with) a married person? A skank, that's who.

This "person" will be sweet and fun and spoil the kids. She'll be wonderful and cool.

Compared to her, you will be a nag and totally uncool.

There's nothing you can do about this. The court-shocker-doesn't care. It's not illegal and, in most states, has no bearing on the divorce settlement.

Do not ask the narc to keep his new woman away from the kids. He'll love you asking because he knows you're upset.

Do not have any contact with the skank (and, don't call her the skank to the kids). You don't have to deal with her. Skanks love it when the wife talks to them; it is entertainment for them.

If she stays with the narc after the divorce, you'll have to deal with her. But not until then.

Don't talk badly about this woman to the kids, but tell them the truth: "What dad and Bambi are doing is sin. The Bible calls it adultery. I don't care, but God does."

CHAPTER SEVENTEEN

The Legal War: Mistakes to Avoid

As you enter this legal war, keep this message in mind:

The Lord is my light and my salvation-whom shall I fear? The Lord is the stronghold of my life-of whom shall I be afraid? When evil men advance against me to devour my flesh, when my enemies and my foes attack me, they will stumble and fall. Though an army besiege me, my heart will not fear; though war break out against me, even then will I be confident. (Psalm 27:1-3)

Remember that you are not alone in this war. You have your human warriors. But most importantly, you have God. God will be with you all the way to the end.

Don't Think the narc Will Be Reasonable

The narc will act reasonable at times, but reasonable is the last thing he's going to be. He will be cruel and vicious and vindictive.

The narc wants to win. He has to win. He will leave you with ten cents and sleep at night. In fact, he'll feel like he got cheated.

The narc believes everything belongs to him: the money, your home, your vehicles, your possessions, his business, all the assets, and the children. It's all his and you are entitled to exactly none of it.

You and your attorney will have to fight hard to pry what you need out of his cold, selfish, despicable hands.

Don't Think You'll Get Justice

You won't get justice. You'll get divorced with the best deal possible and your sanity barely intact. And that's all you're going to get. And you'll have to scratch and claw to get that.

It is not the justice system. It's a system all right, but it has nothing to do with justice. It should be called the *We're Going to Shaft You and We're Going to Get Paid* system.

Ecclesiastes 3:16 is an accurate description of the "justice" system:

And I saw something else under the sun: In the place of judgment-wickedness was there, in the place of justice-wickedness was there.

The legal arena is filled with wickedness. Since the narc is also wicked, he has a distinct advantage. He'll use the system to win and to punish you. And most in the system will be glad to help him.

The court doesn't care about you. The court doesn't care about your children. The court doesn't care about your finances. The court doesn't care about all the abuse you've taken from the narc. The court doesn't care what happens to you.

You are a case number. You are a customer. Nothing more.

God cares about you. Your human warriors care about you. That's it. The callous, jaded, cynical legal professionals only care about checking your case off their list and getting paid.

Don't Be Nice

Nice girls-and guys-lose in the divorce process. Not just most of the time. All of the time.

You have to be cold. You have to be mean. You have to be aggressive. You have to be righteously angry. I'll bet this isn't your personality. Doesn't matter. If you are nice, the narc will wipe you out and laugh his head off while doing it.

You'll have to fake these tough qualities. Fine. Fake them. And make sure your attorney has these qualities.

Avoid these nice actions like the plague:

- Communicating with the narc about the divorce
- Using the same attorney
- Trying the collaborative divorce process

No, no, and no. You are not in an amicable divorce with a decent, normal person. You are in a highly adversarial war with an abusive narc who wants to destroy you.

If you get a protective order against the narc, do not drop it! If there are domestic violence charges against the narc, do not drop them!

Give the narc absolutely no breaks. No mercy. No grace. No generosity. No benefit of the doubt. Use every bit of leverage you can against him.

You and your attorney-who better not be nice, either-must be relentless in a brutal campaign to get a decent settlement.

Show no emotion, except anger. Show no weakness. Go for the jugular.

You and your attorney must play the legal game. And it is a game. A game of:

- Cat and mouse
- Horse trading
- Intimidation
- Shifting strategies
- Stalling
- Negotiation
- Hardball tactics

Don't Try to Prove He's Emotionally Abusive

The narc *is* emotionally abusive. That's why you are divorcing him. But no one-no one-in the legal system cares if he is or not. Even if you could prove it-which you can't-no one cares.

The narc will deny it, of course. So, it's your word against his and he's a fantastic liar. But he could stand up in court and admit to being emotionally abusive, and no one would care.

Don't waste time and energy and money trying to prove he's emotionally abusive. You won't get the vindication you are after and it makes no difference legally.

The court only cares about physical violence-against you or the kids. If you can prove his emotionally abusive behavior puts your kids at risk-it significantly impacts their physical and emotional and educational functioning-the court may care about that.

Don't Hire the Wrong Attorney

I'm repeating myself, but this is worth repeating: do not hire a wimpy, nice, passive attorney. He (or she) will lose and lose badly.

Don't feel bad if you realize you have a sweet, weak attorney. It's a very easy mistake to make. Suck it up, fire the attorney, and find a new one.

You need a family law attorney who is a tiger. A snarling, claws out, back alley fighter. Here's how you find your legal tiger:

- Ask all your friends
- Ask every divorced person you know

- Ask every attorney you know
- Ask experienced therapists
- Ask your family doctor
- If anyone you know works in the legal system (judge, bailiff, paralegal, court reporter), ask them
- If anyone you know has a connection-personal or professional-to a judge, ask them to ask the judge for names
- Ask leaders and attenders in DivorceCare and Celebrate Recovery groups
- Ask local domestic violence and women's centers

Once you have a list of family law attorneys, check out their websites and online reviews. Schedule appointments to interview them.

Find out if the attorney is tough and experienced in dealing with narcs. Ask how she has handled narcs and their slimy attorneys. She should be able to tell you, in detail, her proactive and aggressive plan of action.

Do these interviews asap because many narcs will consult with all the best divorce attorneys in town. That way, if he consults with an attorney before you do, that attorney/firm can't take you as a client-even if he doesn't use them. These consults are worth the fee.

CHAPTER EIGHTEEN

The Legal War: What You Can Do

The legal war is going to be chaotic. Incredibly stressful. Exhausting. Painful. Traumatic. There's no avoiding these harsh realities.

You will be attacked repeatedly. You will be knocked down over and over again. But, take heart and hope from this Bible passage:

... for though a righteous man falls seven times he rises again ... (Proverbs 24:16)

You'll fall many more than seven times. But, with God's power, you'll get back up every time.

You and your mean, I hate narcs attorney do need to respond to the narc's evil, crazy, outrageous legal attacks. (I cover many of these attacks in the next chapter)

But you also need to be proactive. To have a plan and execute it. To stay on the attack.

Here are some essential actions you need to take.

Connect to a Domestic Violence Center

A local domestic violence center can do far more for you than just recommend a tough family law attorney. The staff *will* care about the emotional abuse and will provide practical help.

The center will know the legal reasons you can call the police. For example, in California, the narc can't: grab your phone out of your hand, throw your belongings out into the street or yard, or steal your car keys. You can call 911 and, hopefully, press charges.

You can talk to somebody who has extensive experience in dealing with an abusive narc. Most of the staff, if not all, have personal experience with narcs in their own lives.

These centers have a 24 hour hotline manned by counselors. If you are in crisis mode, you can call and get guidance and support.

Make a Reasonable Offer

Your attorney will offer the narc a reasonable settlement. The message is: "Let's do a fair deal regarding money and custody and save a ton of money on the attorneys."

You express no anger. You make no accusations. You assure the narc that you'll protect his reputation. Some narcs-some-will be reasonable because they want to save their precious money.

Most narcs, however, will reject your offer and remain in attack mode. When that happens, all bets are off and you and your attorney retract the offer and go to war.

Show Only Strength

Your attorney tells the narc's attorney that you will never stop fighting for what is fair. The opposition needs to know you are prepared to take the case all the way to the bitter end, no matter the cost.

All a narc understands is strength. If you show the slightest weakness or hesitation, he will go in for the kill.

Stay on the Attack

You can't afford to be reactive, to only respond to the narc's legal attacks. You and your attorney must be proactive and launch your own attacks:

- Filing motions
- Stalling
- Postponing hearings and mediation meetings at the last minute
- Making offers
- Using leverage
- Threatening to expose unethical and illegal activity of the narc
- Threatening to expose his lies to the court

Use Every Bit of Leverage

Use everything you possibly can against the narc:

- Alcohol, drug, gambling, and sex addiction
- Adultery
- Any unethical or illegal actions the narc has committed on his job
- Unpaid taxes or fraudulent tax returns
- The narc's previous legal convictions

Even if your state courts don't care about these above actions, the narc may not want them revealed in court. And, you are perfectly willing to tell the IRS and his company about his questionable-and probably illegal-financial behavior.

His company will care about him lying on his expense account. If he's involved in an adulterous relationship with a coworker, they'll care about that, too.

Your message, through your attorney, is: "If you agree to a fair deal, none of these issues will be revealed to anyone. If you won't do a deal, they all will be revealed to the court and the proper authorities."

Make Deals for More Custody

Most narcs only want 50-50 custody to save money, punish you, and look good. And for most narcs, money talks.

Using the message, "I think this is best for the kids," offer to take less money in return for more custody/more time/more decision-making with your children.

In return for a better custody deal, you'll take:

- Less child support
- Less retirement money
- Fewer assets

You don't give the farm away, but you do make concessions to get more custody. A better financial deal will make the narc think he's won.

If the narc refuses your deals, take these offers off the table and go to war. Let the narc know the battle for custody and money will cost him a fortune. And you don't care.

Document About the Kids

When you are in the presence of the narc and the kids, document every negative/abusive behavior he inflicts on them:

- The date
- The time
- What happened
- What the narc said and did
- What the child said and did
- What was the result?

Document this same information when your kids tell you about an abusive event they experienced outside of your presence. Even though the narc will spoil them and give them great freedom, he will still be abusive at times.

This information may come in handy in the legal process.

Exchanges

When exchanging the kids with the narc, do two things. One, video the transfer and tell him you are doing it. While this may not be admissible in court, it usually helps keep his rage and verbal abuse under control.

Two, meet at a drugstore for the transfer. Get there first and buy a pack of gum and get the receipt. The receipt will prove you were there when you were supposed to be. The narc won't show up and then will lie and say he was there and you weren't. The receipt will prove he's a liar and protect you.

How to Deal with the Guardian Ad Litem

In many divorce cases involving custody disputes, the court will order a Guardian Ad Litem. This person's job is to protect the children's interests and provide the court with an evaluation and recommendations. The Guardian Ad Litem has a great deal of influence.

Stay calm, composed, and rational with the GAL. Do not attack your spouse and try to get the GAL to see that he is abusive. Do not use the words abuse and narcissist.

If asked, speak the truth-with specific examples-about your spouse's behavior. Use facts, not emotion. Simply report what the narc said and did.

Don't try to be friends with the GAL. Be cordial and respectful. Talk about your kid's needs, their personalities, and how the divorce is hard on them. Give the GAL this consistent message: "I want what's best for my children."

Push Your Attorney

Even when you have an excellent, skilled attorney, you have to be assertive with her. You have to push her to take action. You have to be the squeaky wheel.

Stay on your attorney. Get regular updates. If you feel that something isn't right or you disagree with a course of action, talk to your attorney about it.

CHAPTER NINETEEN

The Legal War: What the narc Will Do

The narc and his nasty, creepy (and almost certainly narcissistic) dirtball of an attorney will throw every legal trick in the book at you.

You and God Against the Philistine

Your human warriors and your attorney are with you. And, you know who else is with you, don't you? 1 Samuel 17:45 tells you:

David said to the Philistine, "You come against me with sword and spear and javelin, but I come against you in the name of the Lord Almighty . . ."

You are also dealing with a Philistine. He will come against you with the intent to destroy you. But you will come against him with the Lord Almighty on your side.

This isn't a complete list, by any means, of what the narc and his loser attorney will throw at you. But here are some of the most common attacks you can expect.

The Lies

He'll tell you he had no idea his attorney made some nasty attack or bogus motion. Liar. The narc knows exactly what his attorney is doing.

He'll beg you to drop your attorney and work only with him to reach a deal:

"I've had a change of heart"... He doesn't have a heart

"God has spoken to me"... Satan has spoken to him

"I want to save money"... True, but he'll save money by taking your money

"I'll be fair"... Fair to himself!

Have your attorney tell his attorney to put this new, "fair" deal in writing and send it over. That will stop this nonsense.

The narc will lie, lie, and lie some more about money:

- He'll lie about his income
- He'll stop working
- He'll fire you from his business
- He'll close down his business
- He'll get a lower paying job

- He'll fake a physical or emotional disability
- He'll hide money and assets
- He'll give money to his relatives
- He'll max out credit cards
- He'll stop paying the mortgage on your home, without telling you, of course
- He'll stop paying bills
- He'll forge your signature to get tax money, to sell your home, to sell your vehicle, to liquidate other assets

It's your attorney's job to expect these moves, expose them to the court, and get consequences applied. Judges don't like to be lied to.

The Cancellations

The narc will secretly cancel everything in sight:

- Your auto insurance
- Your life insurance
- His life insurance
- Your health insurance
- Your credit cards
- Your phone
- Your lawn service, your pest control
- Your kid's private school registration

- Your name off all the bank accounts

Your attorney needs to document all these moves and use them as leverage with the court. Your attorney can subpoena all his bank accounts. Sometimes, a forensic CPA will be needed to sort out all his deceitful financial moves.

The Threats

The narc will bury you in an avalanche of threats. He'll threaten to:

- Get you arrested for a variety of bogus charges
- Get a protective order to take the kids from you
- Get full custody of the kids because you are an unfit mother
- Get your inheritance money
- Leave you with no money
- Get you fired from your job
- Not pay for your attorney
- Come after you for alimony
- Come after your 401K, your Roth, and your savings

Inform your attorney of these threats and give the narc no response.

The Accusations

The accusations will fly during the divorce. The narc will accuse you of:

- Physical and emotional abuse against him
- Physical, emotional, and even sexual abuse against the kids
- Not following the court-ordered parental agreement
- Parental alienation
- Harassment when you reach out to discuss bills, taxes, the kid's needs, and timesharing issues

Share all his accusations with your attorney. It's her job to devise a strategy to refute them. In many cases, a series of counter charges may be in order.

The Refusal to Follow Court Orders

The narc won't follow court orders because no one tells him what to do. This is in your favor, because judges hate it when their orders aren't followed. Your attorney must act swiftly to report these violations and press for contempt of court orders and fines.

The narc won't follow restraining orders, either. Be ready to take a photo or video when he shows up or follows you. Journal all these violations and, of course, report them to your attorney.

The Legal Tricks

The narc and his crumball attorney will use all kinds of legal tricks. Here are some common ones:

- Not getting documents in on time
- Postponing hearings at the last minute
- Not showing up to some hearings
- Filing motion after motion after motion
- Firing his attorneys to drag out the process
- Stalling the divorce to drain your emotional and financial resources
- Not agreeing to anything in mediation
- Trying to get you in the same room with him for mediation
- Agreeing to a settlement and then changing his mind
- Having his attorney attack you in vile ways and ask you terrible things in depositions

Your attorney needs to push back, hard, when these tricks are played. Aggressive counter actions and motions and appeals to the judge are required.

CHAPTER TWENTY

"So Do Not Fear, For I Am With You"

When I am talking to phone advice clients going through a divorce with a narc, I always say: "God is with you."

It's not just a comforting, encouraging thing to say. I take it right from the Bible. Read these words spoken by God himself:

"So do not fear, for I am with you; do not be dismayed, for I am your God. I will strengthen you and help you; I will uphold you with my righteous right hand." (Isaiah 41:10)

God speaks these words directly to you.

My Plan

I have given you a manual to guide you through the divorce. My content comes from my community: my in person clients over the years, my phone advice clients, the readers of my books on narcissism and abuse, my YouTube and TikTok and podcast and Instagram and Facebook followers.

What I have shared with you comes from their experiences in divorcing narcs. They have been where you are going.

The divorce war will be awful. It will be a nightmare. It will be the hardest thing you've ever faced in your life. But **IT WILL BE WORTH IT.**

God Gets It

God knows what you've been through in this marriage. God knows what you'll go through in this divorce.

God sees you. God hears you. God believes you. God loves you. God one hundred percent supports your decision to divorce the narc.

God is With You

With God's constant presence, you will get through the divorce. You will be free. You will be happy. You will have joy. You will have peace.

You will give your children and your children's children an opportunity to break the cycle of abuse in their lives.

God will be with you every inch of every step of the journey of divorce and your new life.

ADDITIONAL RESOURCES

Other Books by David Clarke

20 Lies That Keep You With Your Abuser: Reclaiming Your Identity, Your Worth in Christ, and Your Freedom

Enough is Enough: A Step-by-Step Plan to Leave an Abusive Relationship with God's Help with William G. Clarke

I Didn't Want a Divorce, Now What? How to Deal with Your Ex and Your Kids, Heal, and Get a Re-set with William G. Clarke

My Spouse Wants Out: How to Get Angry, Fight Back, and Save Your Marriage with William G. Clarke

I Destroyed My Marriage: How to Win Your Spouse Back with William G. Clarke

Married But Lonely: Seven Steps You Can Take With or Without Your Spouse's Help with William G. Clarke

I Don't Want a Divorce: A 90-Day Guide to Saving Your Marriage with William G. Clarke

What to Do When Your Spouse says, "I Don't Love You Anymore": An Action Plan to Regain Confidence, Power and Control with William G. Clarke

A Marriage After God's Own Heart

The Secret to Becoming Soulmates: A Couple's Devotional Journey to Spiritual Intimacy with William G. Clarke

Kiss Me Like You Mean It: Solomon's Crazy in Love How-To Manual with William G. Clarke

I'm Not Ok and Neither Are You: The 6 Steps to Emotional Freedom with William G. Clarke

Men Are Clams, Women Are Crowbars: The Dos and Don'ts of Getting Your Man to Open Up with William G. Clarke

Parenting is Hard and then you die: A Fun but Honest Look at Raising Kids of All Ages Right with William G. Clarke

Honey, We Need to Talk: Get Honest and Intimate in Ten Essential Areas with William G. Clarke

Adult Children Who Break Your Heart: Bringing Your Prodigal Back to God and Back to You

To order Dr. Clarke's books, set up a telephone advice session, and access his podcast and his YouTube Channel and other social media platforms, go to:

    davideclarkephd.com

    Or

    davideclarkephd@gmail.com

ABOUT THE AUTHOR

David E. Clarke, Ph.D., is a Christian psychologist, podcaster, YouTuber, TikToker, and the author of seventeen books including, *Enough is Enough: A Step-by-Step Plan to Leave an Abusive Relationship with God's Help* and *I Didn't Want a Divorce, Now What? How to Deal with Your Ex and Your Kids, Heal, and Get a Re-set.*

He is a graduate of Dallas Theological Seminary in Dallas, Texas and Western Conservative Baptist Seminary in Portland, Oregon. He and his beautiful Blonde, Sandy, live in Tampa, Florida. They have four children and five grandchildren.